VERSION CHANGES

V1.0 Original Version

DISCLAIMER

This guide is meant to be used for educational purposes only and should not be substituted for financial advice. I am not your financial advisor or your lawyer. If you want professional financial advice or tax advice, please seek a licensed specialist. I am simply stating my opinion of how finances and investing should be handled. My opinions and strategies may work for me, but there is no guarantee that it will work for you.

TABLE OF CONTENTS

Introduction 1

Chapter 1: 16 Principal Steps To Financial Freedom 7

Chapter 2: Path To Financial Freedom 135

Chapter 3: Side Hustles 137

Chapter 4: X Factor/Owning Your Own Business/Interview With Business Owners 143

Chapter 5: Financial/Money Saving Tips 153

Chapter 6: Tax Tips 175

Chapter 7: Life Tips 183

Chapter 8: Legacy Protection 189

Conclusion 193

Acknowledgements 197

Index And List Of Recommended Financial Tools/Accounts/Websites Throughout The Guide 198

Book References 205

INTRODUCTION

Let me give you a quick explanation of who I am and why I am writing this book. I am a 23-year-old recent college graduate with a computer engineering degree. I work for a company called Manhattan Associates making 69 thousand dollars a year. During the last year of college, the school I went to decided they were going to cut financial aid. This left me in a situation where I needed to come up with five thousand dollars within a year. I am not a person to allow anything to beat me, I will challenge anything in life even if it results in failure, so I started reading up on small businesses and finances, I literally read every piece of literature and media I could get my hands on. I easily read over 100 finance books within a year, trying to obtain as much information as possible. I was absolutely infatuated with investing, business, and finance.

During my absurd rate of consumption of financial information, I took extensive notes on the similarities between books and ignored the information that seemed like it was heavily opinionated or outright wrong. After doing as much research on the topic as humanly possible within a year, I started to formulate a foolproof plan to master money and finances and become financially free and financially independent. I never wanted to be in a position where I was controlled by money again.

I started a small eBay business to pay the five thousand dollars over the next coming year so I could stay in school and get my computer engineering degree. Not only did I make 5k within that year, but also I nearly cleared almost 10k in profit. I finally understood what my parents have been telling me my whole life, and that was that anything is possible if you are willing to put in the blood, sweat, tears, and hard work to make it happen.

This book is the combination of many years of personal struggle, knowledge from over 250+ pieces of financial, investing, or business-oriented media compacted and made concise with omission of opinionated or outright bad advice. I have created an easy step-by-step guide that anyone dedicated to making a change can follow and succeed with. The steps that I have created are called the 16 steps to financial freedom and independence.

This book contains a detailed easy-to-follow plan to reach financial freedom and independence. It will make you realize that the only thing that can stop you from reaching your financial goals is a lack of knowledge and commitment. The concept of committing yourself to something and putting in the work to achieve your goals applies not only to finances, but also every facet of life. If you create a plan and continually execute it, you can't help but to become successful at what you want to do.

This book is not designed to cater to people who do not know what they want for themselves financially. If you are unsure on what you want financially for yourself or you are not 100% dedicated to becoming financially free and independent, go read Dave Ramsey's book, *The Total Money Makeover,* first, then come back to read this book. His guide sacrifices money, time, and resources to give you a psychological edge to help you reach your financial goals. The purpose of this book is to create the most efficient, sound, and quickest way to achieve financial goals while being clear and concise. I might be a bit biased here having written this book and all, but I believe you will not find a more efficient, clear, and concise book on reaching financial independence and freedom.

This book is full of links to other websites that provide more in-depth details on a subject that I cannot or will not elaborate on. This provides me the opportunity to keep this book clear and concise by using external sources to provide additional details. I have also provided plenty of graphs and tables to break up the continuity nature of the book and to help emphasize and drive home some points. Let's be real, who doesn't like a book filled with a couple of graphs, tables, and pictures? I know I do and that is why I included some in this book.

To provide a summary of content you can expect in this book, we will discuss what mindset you will need in order to control money instead of money controlling you, how to get out of debt, how to acquire a better job that pays well, how to build credit, how to properly create a budget, how to buy a house, how to invest, what to invest in, what allocation to invest with, a comprehensive step-by-step guide to acquire financial freedom and independence, life tips, financial tips, tips on how to save more money, how to build generational wealth, and how to protect yourself and your money. This book's goal is to leave absolutely no ambiguity when it comes to anything that is related to finances, money, and what it takes to become an everyday millionaire.

Let me briefly explain what financial Independence and Freedom is and why it should be the goal of every human being that cares about finances. If you are financially independent and free, you are in control of money instead of money being in control of you. Being financially independent means that you have zero debt, no mortgage, and more passive income coming in than expenses every month. If you are financially independent, you don't have to work a job if you don't want to; however, you still must be cautious of how much money you spend and must stay on a budget in order not to work. Being financially free is possessing a passive income amount so large, that it replaces the income that you were getting when you were working your job. Being financially free means you don't have to follow a budget anymore or worry about money, you can do anything that you want to do without going into debt.

What if I told you that you wouldn't have to work after 10-15 years of smart money management? You would probably look at me like I'm crazy, right? What if I told you that it's quite simple and anybody can do it, if you have common sense, dedication, and persistence? I can almost guarantee that you will be a multi-millionaire if you use this guide as a base for your investing. This guide was created to give a clear and concise plan to reach financial freedom and independence. Unfortunately, this knowledge is not taught in school, college, and life. This guide contains everything you need to get started on your path to financial freedom and independence. This guide, however, will not go into exhaustive detail about each of the subjects that I will cover. I will link you to a source that will go into detail about subjects that I cannot cover due to the concise nature of this guide. After you place into effect the steps of this book, the only thing that will be keeping you from being financially free will be yourself.

Getting rich is not as hard as everybody makes it seem; all you need is dedication, a well-written budget, and the persistence to delay instant gratification. America has brainwashed its citizens to believe that you always must have a bigger house and nicer car than you can afford. They give you the option to overleverage yourself with credit cards, handing out mortgages to people they know can't afford it and giving car loans to people who are broke. Americans are addicted to the concept of instant gratification.

Remember when your grandmother said good things come to those who "wait."? Your grandmother wasn't bullshitting when she said this, and she said this because she is wise and knows the truth. If you are addicted to instant gratification, you will have to change your mindset to learn how to appreciate the small things in life instead of relying on outside things such as instant gratification and similar forces. Almost every goal that someone has for themselves is gained by delaying instant gratification.

Let's look at a couple of scenarios where this applies:

Someone wants to lose 50 pounds and get a six-pack, and in order to accomplish this, a person will have to ignore the instant gratification of eating sweets and not working out. The same logic applies to money; you can't expect to get rich or financially free if you keep buying things you can't really afford and are not saving, investing, or putting money towards your passion and your dreams.

No matter your current circumstance, you can achieve financial independence and financial freedom. Believe it or not, if you were raised in a low-income neighborhood, you already possess many of the qualities needed to become financially independent and financially free. Being raised in a low-income area provides skills such as money management, living on less than you have, determination, and discipline. Most of these skills are gained through necessity, but nonetheless these are skills that you possess that someone who was raised in a higher-income area may not have.

CHAPTER 1
16 PRINCIPAL STEPS TO FINANCIAL FREEDOM

The purpose of this chapter is to create a clear and concise 16-step guide to Financial Freedom. You will also obtain Financial Independence along the way to your goal. This goal was created from personal experience and compacting over 100+ financial guides into an easy-to-follow step-by-step guide to reach your goal. These steps account for almost all the different steps of your journey towards Financial Freedom. By following this guide, you will have more money than you will ever know what to do with. You will not have to work a job and you can be worth more than a million dollars easily.

These steps encompass how to get a better job, increase your credit score, get out of debt, set up a budget, set up an investment plan, pay off your house, acquire rental properties, and start your own business. There are a couple optional steps within these 16 Principal steps towards financial freedom. You can choose to do the optional steps if you desire to, but they may slow your progress towards Financial Freedom. The skills that you will gain by reading and following these skills will be ones that will make you financially literature.

To be financially literate means that you know how to properly invest, save, budget, and handle money. You ever heard of people from extremely low-income neighborhoods winning the lottery only to be miserable and lose all the money they gained? This is what happens when you are not financially literate; money controls you instead of you controlling money.

Ever heard the saying that if you were to take all the money away from the richest people in the world, they would find a way back to become rich again? The reason why this is true is because these people have mastered being financially literature. It's amazing how easy it is to make money once you have mastered financial literacy.

The next page contains the 16 steps to financial freedom; please don't skip any section unless marked optional. Even though you may feel like you already know the section, you will be surprised how much information you can learn about something that you feel you have already mastered.

16 PRINCIPAL STEPS TO FINANCIAL FREEDOM

1. Obtain a skill/education that makes financial sense
2. (Optional) Serious financial issues/Over 100k in non-student loan debt
3. Building up your credit
4. Creating a Smart Money Budget
5. Match Companies' 401k Match
6. Move in with relatives or as many roommates as possible
7. Save half a month's income in your bank account
8. Get rid of car payment
9. Revised Debt Plan
10. Rainy Day Fund
11. Invest 15-25% in Investment Portfolio
12. Get 10-20% of down payment on starter home
13. Get 10-year mortgage and make double payments
14. Real Estate Plan to generate a passive income stream
15. (Optional) Time to catch up to the Joneses with their broke ass
16. Repeat Steps 11 and 13 until you become financially free and give back

STEP 1
OBTAIN A SKILL/EDUCATION THAT MAKES FINANCIAL SENSE

If you make less than 50 thousand dollars a year, you need to get a trade/skill/education that makes financial sense or negotiate a raise to get you above the 50k mark. If you plan to negotiate a raise, I'll provide a link below that I used as a basis when I asked for a raise at my job:

Link to negotiating a raise: http://techgenix.com/negotiating-a-raise/

What I mean by a trade/skill/education that makes sense is to get an annual income-to-student debt ratio that is at least two to one. The general rule is that the amount of debt that you go into for the skill/trade/education should not exceed 50% of your expected annual salary. For example: If you go get a Computer Engineering degree with an expected annual salary of $70k, you should not exceed more than $35k in student loan debt. I just want to state that not everyone is cut out for college; however, that doesn't mean that you are destined to make less money than someone who does go to college. There is absolutely zero shame going to trade school to become an AC repair man, electrician, or plumber, for example.

A lot of the time, you end up in a better financial situation compared to someone who went to college if you choose the right profession. If you choose to go the trade school route, you will accrue little student loan debt with the potential to make more money than most people with college degrees! It also is an easy avenue to start up your own business later, but we will get more into that topic in a later chapter.

If you plan to go to college to get a degree, I highly suggest that you go to community college or a local small college for your core classes first. The reason why I recommend this is because almost all major colleges and universities allow you to roll over your core classes to another school. Taking your core classes at a different cheaper school will allow you to save thousands of dollars. A lot of the time, these hard core classes will be easier compared to taking them at the other school. Typically, some of your hardest classes are core classes, so it makes sense to take easier versions of them for a fraction of the money.

After finishing all of your core classes, your GPA should be relatively high, and it will be a lot easier to get into your dream school. This is not only because you have a higher GPA, but also it's a general rule that transferring to another college, when you have finished some college classes is much easier.

If you plan to go to college an additional tip to save some money on textbooks is that you can find most of them online for free, especially for core classes. I also recommend splitting a book or borrowing a book from someone who is in your class or has taken the class already. It is not like when your mom and dad were in school, where they had to pay for textbooks because there was no other option. The age of the internet has made getting textbooks a lot easier. Please reference the Website and Book Link at the end of this book, because it includes a link that I used while in college to find cheap or free textbooks.

If you plan to go the trade route, make sure to take classes where you can practice doing the skill instead of just taking classes online. It's okay to take some online classes for your trade, but please make sure to get some hands-on experience as well. This will allow you to get real-world experience and build connections with people in the field, which is more likely to get you a job compared to just taking online classes.

Once you get your certification, try and find yourself an apprenticeship if you cannot find a job outright. This will allow you to expand on your newly acquired craft while getting paid. The flexibility of going to trade school opens the doors to you owning your own business in the foreseeable future, because once you become a master at your trade, you can easily open up your own business to sell your skills.

Below is a list of jobs that require a degree or trade school certification that I know meets our criteria of acquiring a job that makes financial sense. These jobs typically have around or higher than a 50k salary. There are obviously other jobs that meet our criteria besides the ones listed below, the below table is merely to give you a few suggestions. I don't care what job you get, as long as it has a salary of or around 50k.

Before we look at the jobs that make financial sense, I must first go on a slight rant. I don't want to hear that you don't have time to go get the training for a better job. I don't care if you have five kids and you work a tiresome job, if you don't have time to better yourself and go to night school or online school, I can't help you. You need to first go read a book about motivation and time management. Once you are committed to doing whatever possible to become financially free and independent, nothing can stop you from reaching your financial goals.

JOBS THAT MAKE FINANCIAL SENSE
(F.S=Financial Sense)

Degrees that make F.S	Trades that make F.S
Engineering	Plumbing
Computer Science	Construction/Equipment Operation
Medicine/Biology	Ac Repair Man/Electrician
Nursing	Auto Body Repairmen
Finances/Economics	Elevator Installer/Repairer
Law	Web Developer/IT
Logistics	Dental Hygienist

STEP 2
(OPTIONAL STEP)

Serious Financial Issues/Over 100k in Non-Student Loan Debt

Before I begin, I just want to point out that this is an optional step. And if you don't have serious financial issues or are over 100k in non-student loan debt or close to that, please skip this step and go to step 3. If you meet the above criteria, please don't feel bad that you've made some terrible financial decisions in the past. In fact, according to statistics, I expect over 30% of the readers of this book to need this section. It's okay that you have made some non-wise financial situations, just remember that people develop or go through situations and/or life's stage at different rates. The good news is that you can get out of this situation and there is hope at the end of the tunnel now!

Let's begin with two very realistic financial situations that may occur to someone in their life. Let's name the woman in this situation Taylor. Taylor gets into a good expensive-as-shit private school and accumulates over 100k in student debt and 100k in personal non-student loan debt to get a degree that doesn't fit our criteria of one that makes financial sense. She gets her degree in the school of Liberal Arts or Literal Farts as I like to call it, because all the degrees there literally offer you shit in returns in the category of making money. I'm not saying these degrees aren't needed nor worth getting from an interest point of view; however, it doesn't make sense from a financial point of view. If you are truly passionate about the Liberal Arts, first make a lot of money doing something else that you don't hate, become financially free or independent, then indulge in your interest for the liberal arts, when you don't need to have a job that pays well. Some of these Liberal Arts degrees that pay you jack shit are dancing, drama, women gender studies, psychology, and/or more. I am not trying to offend anyone that has a

Liberal Arts degree, because you may not have had the knowledge at the time to get a degree that makes financial sense.

Let's get back to Taylor. After graduating and not being able to find a "Dancing" job, Taylor lives with her boyfriend and decides to have two kids. The boyfriend eventually leaves her and her children, and Taylor now must get a job. Taylor gets a job as a server at a decent restaurant, where she manages to make around 10 dollars an hour; however, this is not enough money to take care of herself and her two small children, so she decides to get a second job. Since Taylor and her two kids live below the poverty line, she must depend on food stamps and support from the government for sustenance. You're probably thinking that there is no way I can possibly help Taylor, but you would be wrong. No matter what financial situation you are in, there is something that can be done about it.

The first step of plan that I would tell Taylor to follow is to file for bankruptcy to get rid of her non-student debt. The reason why I would recommend this to Taylor is because unlike student loan debt which will not go away from filing bankruptcy, personal debt will. Using my plan, you will not really need credit for the next five years of your life. This will give you time to repair your credit and possibly improve it past the original point. There are two different options when it comes to filing for bankruptcy: you can file a chapter 7 or chapter 13 bankruptcy.

When you file a chapter 13 bankruptcy, you begin the process of reorganizing, reducing, and creating a plan to repay your debt. Using this method, you typically pay a fraction of the total debt that you originally had. When you file a chapter 7 bankruptcy, your total non-personal debt is vastly or totally forgiven in certain circumstances; however it can and will destroy your credit temporarily. This is not a major concern for us, because I guarantee that her credit score will be better than it was before we filed for bankruptcy after she follows the steps of this guide to obtain financial freedom.

The process of rebuilding your credit can take up to 10 years; however, I do not expect it to take nearly 10 years. Before you file for bankruptcy, you have to make yourself become committed to the idea of never being in debt again. If you don't change your mindset about money and not wanting to be in debt, you will end up in the same situation you are in now. Let's say Taylor filed a chapter 13 bankruptcy form and has now eradicated her personal debt, the next task that Taylor should focus on is getting rid of her student debt. Taylor will have to make sacrifices over the next two to five years to get herself out of this situation. It will be tough for Taylor over these next few years, but she is going to continue because she remembers the end goal of being out of debt: getting a good job and becoming financially independent and free. Taylor will literally have to run on 4-6 hours for the next year to get out of this situation. Taylor will have to sacrifice half of her sleeping time to go to online school to get herself a trade that makes financial sense which we mentioned in the last section of this guide. It should take Taylor no more than a year to get her certification for her trade.

She will then go out and start looking for work in her trade field. Taylor should be able to find a job within three months and start making over 50k. Now that she is making at least 50k, she will follow the accelerated getting-out-of-debt budget, budget 4 in Step 4 of the guide to financial freedom. It will take Taylor a longer period of time to get out of debt compared to what I have planned out for the average person, but the good news for Taylor is that it is very doable and she will get out of her terrible financial situation if she follows this book.

Let's take the second situation featuring an adult male whose name is Bob. Bob was raised in a traditional low-income neighborhood. Due to his surroundings and the poor educational system, he didn't complete high school. The first step I recommend for Bob is to study for and pass his GED. The GED is a state standardized test that is commonly seen as the equivalent of a high school degree. If you are like Bob and you don't have your GED, please see the links section and click on the link for studying and preparing for the GED. If you study for four hours a week for three months, you will almost certainly pass the GED.

Bob, after studying for three months, passes the GED with flying colors. Bob, with his newly acquired GED, follows this guide and goes to trade school to pursue and get a trade. Same as with Taylor, it should not take Bob more than a year to get his certification. Bob goes out immediately and starts looking for a job or apprenticeship. Bob also has 100k or more in personal debt, so he also files bankruptcy to get out of his personal debt just like Taylor.

Bob, while getting his certification, is working a full-time job to take care of himself. And while working to survive and following this book, he finds time to study online to get his certification for one of the trades that we talked about before. Bob finally lands a job after three months of apprenticeship. Bob follows budget 4 of step 4 and finds himself out of debt within three years.

These are just a couple of mock scenarios of possible financial situations that some people find themselves in. The purpose of using this example is to show you that no matter your financial situation, there is a solution to get you out of it. If you're thinking about filing for bankruptcy or want to know more about it, please check out the links sections for more information about chapter 4 and 13 bankruptcies and how to file for them.

Before you file for bankruptcy, please think about all the consequences beforehand, and seek a financial advisor and/or lawyer to see if bankruptcy makes sense for you. Some of the consequences of filing for bankruptcy include making it near impossible to get a mortgage, credit card, and the fact that creditors will try and sell most, if not all, of your assets to try and reclaim some of the money that you owe them.

STEP 2
START BUILDING CREDIT

Before we discuss how to properly build credit, a lot of you are probably wondering why we are talking about Credit Cards. Dave Ramsey and other financial advisors say that you don't need, and you shouldn't get, a credit card! I understand why financial advisors, such as Dave Ramsey, say one shouldn't own a credit card. Credit cards, for people with poor financial skills, is like putting a piece of chicken in front of a dog and telling them not to eat it. I agree that people who are not financially literate with money management shouldn't have a credit card. I am under the assumption that you will read this book and follow each of the steps towards financial freedom and independence religiously. Reading this book and following this guide will teach you to become financially literate.

Now that we've addressed the elephant in the room, let's start looking under what circumstances and rules credit card are beneficial to our goal to financial freedom.

The first rule of credit cards is to never have a balance on your credit card for longer than a month. If you are going to pay interest on your credit cards, don't get one and take the Dave Ramsey approach to credit, which is not owning credit cards and ignore your credit score. Rule 2 of credit cards is to treat your credit card like a debit card. This means you should never spend more money than you have in your bank account and on your budget.

We are going to shoot for a credit score of 680 at first, because this is when you start getting lower interest rates and getting a loan becomes easier. Our final credit score target is 760, because after that, there is no difference between 760 and a perfect score of 850. Anything after 760 is reserved purely for bragging rights.

(Link to Dave Ramsey approach to credit cards)

https://www.daveramsey.com/blog/the-number-one-way-credit-score

For people who swear to never pay interest on a credit card, it's time to start building up your credit while you are getting your degree and skill. I recommend getting a student credit card with a low balance if you can. Or if your credit is shit, get a credit card where you put money on the card before you can use it. This guarantees that you won't ever pay interest on the credit card. Anytime you have any expense that you can put on a credit card, do so and pay it off immediately. This shows credit card companies that you are active and trustworthy. You are also getting 1-3% off on literally almost everything that you buy.

The types of credit cards that I recommend getting are stated below:

The first one is a traveling credit card that has zero foreign transaction fees and superb benefits for traveling. If you travel very often because of a job or out of necessity, using a travel credit card can go a long way towards making your next vacation extremely affordable.

The second credit card I recommend is the generic credit card that gives you a 1.5-2% cashback off on every purchase. If you don't have a credit card that gives a higher than 2% cashback rate for a purchase, use the generic credit card for that purchase.

The third type of credit card that I recommend getting is one for food and gas, since these are necessities and a large part of your monthly expenses. If you plan to get a fourth credit card, I would recommend getting a rotating categories credit card where every month or couple of months, the categories of purchases where you get 3-5% cashback change. I personally don't recommend getting a credit card that has an annual fee, because it makes you feel obligated to hit spending quotas for the credit card to benefit you. They can, however, be beneficial if you are diligent about how you spend your money and/or tend to spend a lot on a certain category that the credit card is offering cashback for.

A lot of the time, I find that keeping up with my spending and making sure that I hit spending quotas are more work than its worth.

Once you have had a credit card for a year, I recommend getting two more credit cards. Your credit score will take an initial hit, but the credit inquiries will drop off your credit report before the time you will need credit. Every six months, call your credit card company and ask if they can raise your balance limit on your credit card. Set up automatic payments on your credit cards for every month to make sure that you never pay interest. If you follow these steps, you will have an excellent credit score in no time; this will apply later when you are getting mortgages for rental properties.

I want to quickly talk about balance transfers credit cards and how or if they would be beneficial to you. If you owe 10,000 dollars or more on a credit card with a high interest rate and you are in the process of paying it off, it might be beneficial to use a balance transfer credit card to do so. If you were to get a balance transfer credit card with a fee of 3% that has an introductory rate of 0% interest for the first year and you are determined to pay off your credit card balance in full within the introductory period, it would be worth it to open a balance transfer credit card. In the scenario above, you essentially traded paying 15-25% compounding interest monthly for a one time fee of $300 dollars. Please also be considerate of the balance limit on the new card, because if it is lower, that can affect your credit score. I'll leave a link below that's a calculator that determines if a balance transfer makes sense for you: https://www.creditcards.com/calculators/balance-transfer/

If you want to know what credit cards you should get or why, please click the link below to go to the credit card section of this guide below: https://www.creditkarma.com/auth/logon

I recommend using credit karma to keep track of your two scores and as a reference for the best credit cards you can get. I want to briefly talk about a common misconception about credit cards, It's a myth that checking your credit score will make it go lower. I check it daily and it has never gone down once. If you already have bad credit, I suggest paying off the credit cards you have and never ever carry a balance again. If you have terrible credit, I would also recommend that you pay some money to get Lexington law to remove some of the dings against your credit. I promise you that your 400-dollar investment into Lexington Law will be well worth it when you are saving literally tens of thousands of dollars in interest over your lifetime, because you fixed your credit.

Link to Lexington law is below:

https://www.lexingtonlaw.com/

STEP 3
MAKE A SMART MONEY BUDGET

Budgeting, making a budget, and sticking to it are the most important and hardest part of the 16-step guide to financial independence. A good budget is the difference between a person who is building generational wealth and one who is keeping up with the Joneses. The term "Joneses" refers to anybody who would rather spend every cent of their disposable income to keep up with the image that they are rich and wealthy when, in reality, they are 100-300 thousand dollars in debt. Even though the statement, "budgeting is the hardest part of the 16-step plan to financial independence", it doesn't mean that it's not achievable. You will have to be dedicated and have the willpower in order to stick to your budget. What it takes is the willingness to sacrifice unnecessary luxuries such as going out every weekend, spending 100 dollars at a club, buying Yeezies or Gucci, leasing or buying a brand new car, or getting a place that costs way too much money. These things may seem like necessities to you, but they are not. If it is not directly keeping you alive, or giving you a place to lay your head, then it isn't considered a necessity.

In your budget, there will be some room for luxuries, because you have worked hard and deserve to enjoy some aspects of life. I can almost guarantee you that it will not be to the extent that you are currently used to, but you will quickly adjust to your new standard of living. As you work and gain more experience and get paid more over the course of you reading and implementing this guide, you will increase the standard of your life and also keep the same budget that you originally started the guide with. This will allow you to reach financial freedom quicker and faster by allowing you to invest and pay off debt quicker. The average annual pay raise is 3% for jobs that require a college degree. I understand that it will be tempting to increase your spending because you got a pay raise, but you will not change your budget just because you are starting to make more and more every single year. The only circumstances to where you can change your budget are relocation, having kids, marrying, job loss, or major illness.

Now that I have talked about all the pre-requisite information that you need to know before making a budget, let's begin. To start off, our budget is different from a standard budget because we will budget and plan for as many likely life situations as humanly possible. They are likely to happen, so we might as well budget and plan for them and not be surprised when they happen. It goes back to the saying that is most applicable to this book, "If you fail to plan, you plan to fail."

Things that most budgets don't have or consider include car repair cost, house repair cost, travel, and a wiggle room section where if you go over your budget for an area it's planned for.

Let's briefly talk about health insurance, because it can be one of the sections that eats the most money from your budget. Getting a cheaper plan and putting money into a HSA typically comes out cheaper than a more expensive health insurance plan if you rarely get sick. This, of course, depends on the type of health insurance plan that you have currently or that your company provides. This will keep you motivated to stick to the budget and give you something to look forward to at the end of the month. I recommend that if you are a relatively healthy person and you don't have any dependents (kids or people who depend on you), get the cheapest health insurance policy and put $50-100 in a HSA monthly.

A HSA is like a tax-free account that you can put money into to pay for any medical-related cost that you have. I will talk about this in a later section. If you currently have car payments and it's hurting your budget, don't worry, there is a section later to help you eliminate your car payments as quickly as possible. If you have a car payment and/or lease, or if you owe more than 60% on the car's original lease or cost at purchase,

I recommend selling the car to pay off the remainder of the car loan and get yourself a used car for $1500-3000 dollars that will last you till you pay off your debt. This will include buying a cheap temporary car to save money and reduce your monthly expenses. If you have room in your budget, you should save double the monthly allocated "car repairs" to save for a new car, because eventually your used/temporary car will eventually die, and you don't want to remove money from your emergency or rainy-day fund to buy a new car.

Now that I've talked to the point of ad nauseam about prerequisites for budgets, lets look at an actual budget, the example below is my budget:

I need to address a couple of things about my budget before we look at it: I am currently living with my parents; I live far from work about an hour away. I also make 69k a year with a used paid-off car. I am, while paying off debt, only putting 6% of my monthly checks towards my 401k to get the match that my company offers. I am also only making a $100 contribution to my Roth IRA, because I am paying off debt. I have good health insurance provided through my job. I understand this may not be a realistic expectation for everyone, so I will make several budgets to make it applicable to as many people as possible.

In order to making budgeting easier, I recommend using the mint app for android and IOS, as it makes keeping track of your budget 10x easier. The app will ask you to link your bank accounts and credit cards, and as you make transactions on these linked accounts, it keeps track of what you have spent money on and how much for each section of your budget, automating it.

I will link a guide on how to set up your mint account to accurately reflect your budget. The below link is used to set up a budget using Mint: https://www.mint.com/budgeting-3/how-to-cre-ate-a-budget-using-mint

Example of my Budget:

Monthly Income after 401k contributions and health insurance contributions: $3950

Auto Insurance: $95

Gas and Fuel: $200

Student Loans: $300

Entertainment: $25

Groceries: $150

Gas: 150

Restaurants: $50

Gym: $30

Car Repairs: $100

Travel: $100

Health and Beauty aka haircut: $25

Roth IRA Contribution: $100

Wiggle Room: $ 100

Clothing: $25

Total Monthly Income ($3950) – Total Month Expenses ($1300) = $2500

The remaining amount, $2500, in this case, is what you will use to pay off debt, pay off your house, pay off your rental property, and invest. I will talk about each of these things in more detail later on in this guide.

If you remember the definition of financial independence, it's to have more passive income coming in; in this case (total monthly income) than (your monthly expenses). So, in the case of my budget, if you have more passive income than $1300 dollars, you are financially independent.

I had 35 thousand dollars of debt when I graduated college and my plan was to pay it off within a year and a half. I planned to pay it off within one year, which is why I am putting $2800 dollars towards student loans. I just want to quickly state that after I pay off debt, my contributions to my 401k and Roth IRA will go up significantly.

Example 2: Mock Budget of someone living with two roommates that makes 60k a year

Monthly Income $3425

Auto Insurance: $100

Health Insurance: $100

Rent and Utilities for a 3-bedroom two-bath with two roommates: $600

Student Loans: $300

Entertainment: $25

Groceries: $150

Gas: 150

Restaurants: $50

Gym: $30

Car Repairs: $100

Travel: $100

Phone Bill: $50

Health and Beauty aka haircut: $100 Roth IRA Contribution: $100

Wiggle Room: $100

Clothing: $25

Total Monthly Income ($3425) – Total Month Expenses ($1805) = $1355

The remaining $1355 is what you will use to pay off debt, pay off your house, pay off your rental property, and invest. I will talk about each of these things in more detail later on in this guide.

Example 3: Mock Budget of someone living with two roommates that makes 50k a year with a trade

Monthly Income: $2850

Auto Insurance: $100

Health Insurance: $100

Rent and Utilities for a 3-bedroom two-bath with two roommates (Including Utilities): $600

Entertainment: $25

Groceries: $150

Restaurants: $50

Gym: $30

Car Repairs: $100

Gas: $150

Travel: $100

Phone: $50

Health and Beauty: $100

Roth IRA Contribution: $100

Wiggle Room: $100

Clothing: $25

Total Monthly Income ($2850) – Total Month Expenses ($1575) =

$1024

The remaining amount, $1024, is what you will use to pay off debt, pay off your house, pay off your rental property, and invest. I will talk about each of these things in more detail later on in this guide.

These budgets are made to have some leeway to still have a good quality of life. You can eat well and still have some fun on the weekend and even invest some while you work through the 16 steps to financial independence.

Example 4: Mock Budget for someone who is currently in step 2 with a 50k income

Monthly Income: $2850

Auto Insurance: $100

Health Insurance: $200

Rent for a one-bedroom apartment: $1000

Internet/TV: $100

Electricity (Includes stove, ac, water header):

Entertainment: $0

Groceries: $200

Restaurants: $0

Gym: $0

Car Repairs: $100

Gas: $150

Travel: $0

Phone: $50

Health and Beauty: $100

Roth IRA Contribution: $0

Wiggle Room: $ 50

Clothing: $0

Total Monthly Income ($2850) - Total Monthly Expenses ($1800) = $915

If you are following the above budget, you may be currently trying to get out of a terrible financial situation. I don't want to sugarcoat this, you will have to make sacrifices in order to get out of your predicament. This means luxuries that were afforded in budgets 1-3 will not be applicable to this budget. This means no money will be allocated towards entertainment, restaurants, gym, travel, Roth IRA contribution, or clothing and our wiggle room area for overages in our budget is cut into half. Thankfully, you'll only have to stick to this budget until you get below 50k in student debt. Once you have achieved that luxury, you can move to budget 1,2,3,5 or whatever budget best meets your needs at that time.

I do understand if you have two kids or more and you don't want to have roommates. I also understand that not everybody has relatives that they can stay with, but for this budget I am expecting that you will be living by yourself. The reason why I included all typical appliances that run on gas is because, typically, most apartments' appliances run on electricity instead of gas. If you're in an apartment, random utilities, such as water and garbage disposal services, are included, which is why I didn't include it in the above budget.

As always, every single penny of the extra money in your budget after expenses will go towards paying off your student loans or personal debts. In order to pay off debt quicker, I recommend getting one of the many side hustles mentioned in the side hustle section of this guide. If you need a side hustle, try to generate an additional $1000 a month to help pay off your student loans in half the time. You'll have to make sacrifices in order to achieve the goals of this book, but please know that it can be done, and if you need motivation or you need to talk to someone, you can always reach out to me at: jordancoleman12@gmail.com.

Example 5: Mock Budget for someone at the stage of paying off their starter home with increased salary of 50k to 55k after annual raises and raising our 401k contribution from 6% to 15%.

Monthly Income: $2820

Auto Insurance: $100

Health Insurance: $200

Double payment for start home: $1800-$700 dollars for a roommate= $1100

Internet/TV: $100

Electricity (Includes stove, ac, water header): $250

Entertainment: $50

Groceries: $200

Restaurants: $50

Gym: $30

Car Repairs: $100

Gas: $150

Travel: $100

Phone: $50

Health and Beauty: $100

Roth IRA Contribution: $100

Wiggle Room: $ 50

Clothing: $50

Home Insurance: $50

Kids' college tuition savings: $100

Monthly Income ($2820) - Monthly Expenses ($2730) = $90

You'll have to get a roommate while you pay off your starter home, but it will be well worth it when you get additional 600-800 dollars that can go towards rent. You can put the additional $90 dollars towards a portfolio diversification plan. Over the next five years, you will get, on average, an additional 15% while you pay off your house, which will bring your total annual income to $63,200 dollars. This will give you enough money to kick out your roommate and live by yourself or with your wife.

Example 6: Mock Budget for someone who is now financially independent and is working towards financial freedom. This person started out with a 50k job and has had a 45% raise over the 15 years it took to become financially free and is getting a bigger house and a 15% contribution to 401k.

Monthly Income: $3600

Auto Insurance: $100

Health Insurance: $150

1.5 times payment of bigger home: $2800*1.5 = $4200-$2400 from monthly passive income from rental property = $1800

Internet/TV: $100

Electricity (Includes stove, ac, water header): $250

Entertainment: $50

Groceries: $250

Restaurants: $50

Gym: $30

Car Repairs: $150

Gas: $150

Travel: $150

Phone: $100

Health and Beauty: $100

Roth IRA Contribution: $100

Wiggle Room: $ 100

Clothing: $50

Home Insurance: $50

Kids' college tuition savings: $150

Monthly Expenses ($3600) - ($3505) = $20 leftover in the budget to put towards portfolio diversification

One last thing, when you have kids, from the day they are born, add a new section to your budget which allocates $100 in each parent's budget or $200 if you share a budget for each kid every month in a 529 state government's plan. You brought that kid into the world and you are responsible for taking care of them meaning you should pay for their college tuition. The 529 state college plan allows you to contribute tax-free and spend it tax-free as long as you use it for educational purposes.

Please see the below link for more information about the 529 college saving plan. Make sure that your state provides a 529 plan as well. Most states do provide a 529 state plan, but please check if they do.

https://www.savingforcollege.com/intro-to-529s/what-is-a-529-plan

STEP 4
ALWAYS MATCH THE FULL AMOUNT THAT YOUR COMPANY OFFERS

If you don't work for yourself but work for a corporation or business, they more than likely will have some type of retirement plan. Even though you may be in debt and should be eliminating debt like it is the black plague, we will not leave money on the table. Always match what your company is offering to match. For example, my company matches 50% up to 6% essentially a 3% match program. This is 100% guaranteed return on your money and this beats any practical investment or interest rate you have on any loans.

If you are self-employed, save 5% of your annual salary for any incidents or accidents that may occur at your business. Paying off debt is one of the main priorities of this book, but making money and protecting yourself is just as important and you cannot beat a guaranteed 100% return on your money

STEP 5
MOVE IN WITH RELATIVES OR AS MANY ROOMMATES AS POSSIBLE

To save money, pay off debt, and invest more of your money, you will need to move in with your parents or get an apartment or house with as many roommates as you can stand. If you stay at home, you won't have a rent or mortgage bill, but you may have a longer commute to work every single day.

I know living with your parents or roommates isn't sexy or fun, but the sacrifices that you are currently making won't last forever, and it will allow you to get ahead in life. I am recommending that you stay long enough to pay off your debt, save 10-15k, and save for a 10-20% down payment on a starter home. This will allow you to start off life on the right foot with no debt, a rainy-day fund, and enough to correctly buy a house. The time it takes to achieve these three goals will depend on your location, the amount you make, and the amount of debt that you have.

For me, it will take about three years of living with my parents to reach these goals. I promise you that you will feel like a new man or woman once you reach these steps towards financial freedom. Remember that the hardest part of the financial goals is the first half and that it should get easier and easier with each step. It's like working out again after five years; the first workout is the hardest and it will suck ass for the first couple of weeks, but if you keep at it, it will get easier and easier. You will be working out and using your financial muscles by following this guide.

If you live at home, you will save on average 10-20k in rent or mortgage that you would have paid if you lived by yourself. If you live with roommates, you will save on average 6k-8k in rent that you would have paid if you lived by yourself. This can, and will, be the difference that will allow you to reach financial independence and freedom.

STEP 6
SAVE HALF A MONTH'S INCOME IN YOUR BANK ACCOUNT

Before we start paying off debt, you should save half a month of income. This will get you in the state of mind of saving money. Think of it like this, if you can't even save half a month's income, how will you have the discipline to follow this guide and become financially free and independent? This is the time to reinforce the financial muscles that you have been building up to this point. This money is going to be used for emergencies that are not explicitly stated in your budget. Emergencies include overages of car repairs and house repairs, appliance breakdown, medical emergencies, death, and lawsuits or IRS trouble. If you do happen to spend money from your account, make it a priority to pause debt payments, investing, and rental property payments until you fully replace the amount you took out. For example, let's assume you have 2 grand saved up in your bank account and you have a medical emergency where you come out of pocket for 1 grand. For your next paychecks, any excess money left over after your monthly expenses will go to refunding this account to get you back to half a month's paychecks.

Once again, this account is for immediate emergencies only and should not be used for anything besides the scenario stated above. Most financial investors tell you to save 1 grand, which is a good plan, but my plan is slightly different. The beauty of having half a month's expenses is that it will grow as you gain more money and have more expenses that come with having a spouse, kids, etc.

STEP 7
GET RID OF YOUR CAR PAYMENT

Let's start by saying that cars are terrible investments that depreciate every year under normal circumstances. They are a necessary evil, due to the time and age that we live in. Let me begin with the statement that the only thing you should be driving should be a five-year-or-older used car, while you are not at least financially free. If you just bought a new car or if you owe more than 60% on your car, sell it immediately and pay off the remainder of your car loan. Save $1500-3000 dollars and get a used car in working condition. This car may not be the prettiest car on the street or be sexy, but it will get you from point A to point B while you save for a better car. This hooptie car will last you until your debt is paid off and you begin your journey to financial freedom.

I would never ever suggest leasing a car. Leasing is absolutely the most expensive way to own a car. If you currently have a lease, get out of your lease ASAP and buy a used car for the price mentioned above. If you are going over your miles for your lease and they claim to take the miles of the lease if you get another lease, it's a trap to continue the cycle of you leasing more cars. I would suggest biting the bullet and just paying the overage penalty of the miles that you went over for.

The reason why we are getting a used car is because it is the cheapest way to own a car historically and, in our guide, you already know we are all about trying to save every penny possible in order to become financially free and independent. After you pay off debt, save 10-15k in a rainy-day fund, and 10-20% of your down payment, you can buy a newer used car, but not newer than five years from the last model. The reason is that most of the initial overprice cost of a new car is gone within the first five years. This way, someone else is eating the inflated value of the car and you are getting the car closer to what it is worth. I understand if you want a nice Lexus, Mercedes, or Tesla, but this can come later when you have enough passive income to pay for the car payments instead of working a job to pay for it. If you are in the process of selling or buying a car, please use Carfax for the most accurate price estimation so you don't get ripped off either way.

Link to Carfax: https://www.carfax.com/. If you are in the process of buying a used car, please reference this guide below: https://www.consumerreports.org/buying-a-car/used-car-buying-guide/

STEP 8
PAY OFF ALL DEBT USING REVISED DEBT PLAN

Let me start this section by stating the fact that Consumer Debt is a rampant disease in America and it needs to be treated like the black plague. Way too many people ignore debt and pretend like it doesn't exist or that the government is going to forgive it and pay for it. I'm sorry to tell you, but the government is not going to ever take care of it. Our government is extremely broke at the time of writing this book. The United States is currently 17 trillion dollars and counting in debt and the social programs that we currently have now isn't sustainable. I'm not taking a political stance on this issue; all that I stated in the last sentence is 100% facts. These statements are to make you realize that your debt is your responsibility and you will have to take care of it yourself, because that is the only way you will reach financial freedom and independence.

No matter how much debt you are in, I promise you that if you have a plan, you can get out of it. It might take longer than you might like, but it will be worth it when you don't owe anyone. Some of you are probably thinking that they cannot come collect your debts when you're dead. Unfortunately, all your assets that you own that should have been passed on to your kids will be auctioned off to cover as much of your debts as possible. If you have substantial debt that has been building interest year after year after year while not paying down the principal, I can almost guarantee that if you were planning on leaving something to your kids, there will be nothing left after they auction off all your assets.

My debt payment strategy is very similar to Dave Ramsey's Debt Snowball system. If you're not familiar with Dave Ramsey's Debt Snowball, it's the concept of paying off your smallest debts first instead of worrying about paying off the debt with the highest interest rates to keep you motivated to continue paying off debt. This is a great plan if you're assuming that the person paying off the debt will get unmotivated. Once again, I am under the assumption that you are dedicated, motivated, and willing to do whatever it takes to not have to work in 10-15 years and that you are committed to not having to worry about money in 20-25 years if you follow this guide perfectly.

I do want to state that once you have paid off a debt, I would recommend keeping 50 dollars on a loan instead of paying it off, because it may negatively impact your credit score if you completely pay off a loan. You will pay like a dollar in interest a year and that is worth it to keep your credit score about 760. This will allow you to save tens of thousands of dollars on interest when you buy a house.

Below is an example of the difference between Dave Ramsey Debt Snowball and Our Revised Debt Avalanche.

Example of money that you can save using Revised Debt Avalanche

Let's say you have 100k and it will take you five years to pay it off completely.
Let's say, for example, you have 10 loans and you make monthly payments of 2,500:
Loan 1: 3,000 3%
Loan 2: 15,000 6%
Loan 3: 2,000 8%
Loan 4: 7,000 4%
Loan 5: 6,000 4%
Loan 6: 25,000 8%
Loan 7: 14,000 9%
Loan 8: 21,000 7%
Loan 9: 5,000 5%
Loan 10: 2,000 6%

Following Dave Ramsey's advice, you would pay off loan 1,3,4,5,9,10 in year one. If you add up all the interest rates of these loans and weigh them based on their value, you get an interest rate of 5%. If you would have instead started with the highest interest rate of Loan 7: 14,000 and started on Loan 6 after you pay off Loan 7, you would save have saved 4% on the $25,000 thousand dollars loan which amounts to $1250.

The question I pose to you now is, would you rather get the satisfaction of paying off smaller loans or would you rather save $1250 the first year that you are starting to pay off your loans? That's a whole week, maybe two weeks, of additional work that you would have to do because of that satisfaction feeling you like from paying smaller loans off first.

I recommend paying off all of your credit card debt first, private personal loans second, private student loans next, then pay off federal student loans last. The reason why you want to pay your loans off in this order is because, typically, credit card interest rates are the highest, second is private personal loans, third is private student loans, and last is student federal loans. Credit Card interest rates are typically in the high tens or low twenties, private loans are typically in the low tens, private student loans are in the low tens or above 8%, and federal loans are between 3.5% and 6%.

I want you to calculate, using the below link, how long it is going to take you to get debt-free, once we get every part of what we need for our equation. We will use this strategy to calculate how long it will take you to pay off your debt.

First, take your remaining balance from your budget that we created in the budget section. This is the value that is left after you take your monthly income minus your monthly expenses. This value, whatever it is, minus 100 dollars will be what you should be committing to pay off your debts as soon as possible. The reason why it's minus 100 dollars is that you can slowly build up some cash while you pay off debt in your rainy-day fund. For example, if you have $1800 leftover from your monthly budget, you will commit $1700 dollars towards the debt avalanche strategy until you completely pay it off. If you were to get a pay raise at work and you have $1900 dollars leftover in your budget, you would commit $1800 dollars to your debt avalanche strategy.

Below is an example of calculating how long it will take you to pay off your debt. I currently have 19k left at the time of writing this book; it's significantly lower at the time of revising this book, because I live the life I preach. For the concept of consistency, we will use 19k for our example provided below.

Loan 1: $4,320-4.29%

Loan 2: $2170-4.29%

Loan 3: $7700-3.76%

Loan 4: $115-4.450%

Loan 5: $530-04.450%

We will use the strategy of evaluating your effective interest rate by weighing each loan value. In order to accomplish this, you will add up your total loan amount, so in the case of my student loan debt 4320+2170+7700+115+5300= 19605. Divide each loan by this value and multiple by its interest rate and sum up for each value. So for example ((4320/19605) *4.29) + ((2170/19605)*4.29) + ((7700/19605)*3.76) + ((115/19605)*4.45) + ((5300/19605)*4.45) = .9453+.475+1.477+.0261+1.203 = %4.126.

Now that you have your effective interest rate of your total debt combined, take the remaining amount of money left over in your budget after paying your monthly expenses minus 100 dollars, your effective interest rate and your total debt and plug it into the payback calculator provided in the link below.

http://www.finaid.org/calculators/prepayment.phtml. Below is an example of what the above example for 19k would look like

Prepayment Calculator

Making extra payments to reduce the principal balance on a loan can help pay off the loan sooner and reduce the total interest paid over the lifetime of the loan. This calculator shows the impact of making regular extra payments on the loan. It shows the interest savings and the number of payments saved from the repayment schedule as compared with a regular loan that has no prepayment.

Extra Payment may be either a dollar amount or a percentage of the regular monthly payment. For example, to have an extra monthly payment every year specify *Extra Payment* as 100% and *Prepayment Frequency* as Annually.

Loan Balance:	$19605
Interest Rate:	4.126
Loan Term (Years):	20
Extra Payment:	$2500
Prepayment Frequency:	Monthly

CALCULATE

For this example, it will take me seven and a half months to pay off the above debt. Doing the above step will give you a rough estimation of how long you will have to stay in Step 5 of your journey towards financial freedom and independence. The length you need to stay in step 5 is the total time it takes you to pay off debt plus two-three additional years to build up a rainy-day fund and 10-20% on a down payment on a starter home.

Congrats, you have just taken the largest and hardest step of your journey to becoming financially free. Once you have paid off your debt, you no longer owe anyone anything! Most people will never and can never say that. During this process of paying off your debt, your credit score has been increasing, you've gotten used to staying on a budget, and you've been getting paid more and more at work. The hard part is over, and my favorite part is about to begin. As an added bonus, if you were curious.

Below is an Example of how long it will take to pay off my debt:

Prepayment Calculator Results

Loan Balance:	$19,605.00
Loan Interest Rate:	4.13%
Loan Term:	20 years
Regular Monthly Loan Payment:	$120.11
Extra Payment:	$2,500.00
Extra Payment Frequency:	Monthly

Without Extra Payments

Number of Payments:	240
Total Payments:	$28,945.81
Total Interest Paid:	$9,340.81

With Extra Payments

Number of Regular Payments:	8
Cumulative Regular Payments:	$960.88
Number of Extra Payments:	8
Cumulative Extra Payments:	$18,935.93
Overall Total Payments:	$19,896.81
Total Interest Paid:	$291.81

Savings

Prepayment Savings:	$9,048.99
Reduction in Interest:	96.88%
Reduction in Payments:	31.26%
Reduction in Loan Term:	19.3 years (96.67%)

Note: The final extra payment was $1,435.93.

STEP 9
10-15K SAVED IN MONEY MARKET ACCOUNT

Let's begin by talking about how traditional banking accounts are borderline scams. Banks are really ripping you off and are not giving you a fair interest rate at all. Traditional Banks, such as BankAmerica or Wells Fargo, give you maybe 0.1% on a checking account and .25% on a savings account if you're lucky, while charging you $35 dollars every time you don't have enough money in your account to pay for something. This is downright borderline fraudulent and unethical, because they loan out your money that you have in your bank account to charge people anywhere from 4-12% interest while giving you 0.1% or .25% if you're lucky. Thankfully, there is a better solution than keeping money with these legal mobsters. Online banks, in order to be competitive with traditional banks, offer considerably higher interest rates that challenge and sometimes beat the inflation rate.

The reported inflation rate in America is around 1.7%, so if your money market account or savings account doesn't beat 1.7%, you are actively losing money by "Saving" money. This 1.7% is increasing every year and is typically higher than what the government reports in order to prevent mass panic. Some of you are probably asking what a money market account is and how it is different from a savings account. Essentially, they are the same thing; the only difference is that money market accounts don't have as much "Protection on your money" and you are limited to only making six transactions out of your moneymarket account per month. This less protection on your money is a nonfactor and is really only for a doomsday scenario where the bank runs out of money and the United States would literally have to have another great depression in order for this less protection rule to impact you.

The traditional protection on your money in a traditional bank would be up to 250 thousand dollars, which means that the bank would cover your 250k dollars no matter what situation accrued. Online banks and money market accounts typically have around 100 thousand dollars of protection or less, but this depends on the online bank and the money market account that you have. I just want to restate that this scenario is seriously not likely to happen and, in the event, that it does happen, we will have countermeasures to prevent it.

As of the six-transactions-a-month rule that comes with the money market account, this should not be an issue because you shouldn't be taking money out of this account unless it's a dire situation anyway. A dire situation, as I stated before, is death, sickness, loss of job, serious car repairs, house repairs, etc. You can expect around 1% for a checking account and 2-2.5% for a savings/money market account. This is obviously a lot better than what traditional banks offer you with their measly .1% to .25% interest rates.

The only downside of having online banks is that you can't go into a physical location, but since we live in the digital age, why in the world would you willingly walk into a bank? You're probably thinking how to get cash easily if you can't go to a bank. Well, there are tons of free ATMs for any type of card you have. For example, if you're using a MasterCard bank card, most online banks have cards that are MasterCard or Visa. This makes the process of finding a free ATM for your particular card much easier. If you are ready to find a new savings account/checking account, please use the website NerdWallet, and go to savings accounts/money market accounts/checking accounts and choose one that is highly rated and has interest rates comparable to 1% for a checking account and 2-2.5% for a savings/money market account. Please go head and register an account on NerdWallet, because I will reference and use the website a lot in this guide.

Link to Best Checking Accounts: https://www.nerdwallet.com/blog/banking/nerdwallets-top-online-checking-accounts/.

Link to Best Money Market Accounts: https://www.nerdwallet.com/blog/banking/best-money-market-accounts/?trk=nw_gn2_4.0

If you're wondering what checking account/money market account I own, I have a Capital One checking and money market account. The reason why I chose Capital One compared to some other online banks is because I love their customer service and how their company operates. They actually treat you like a customer instead of a number. I could get a higher interest rate at another bank, but the fact that they have good customer service is worth the money I am losing if I were to go with a different bank.

Now that you have a new checking and money market account that is not ripping you off, it's time to start saving cash, invest, and get rich. Typically, financial advisors recommend saving 3-6 months of expenses in your savings accounts; however, out of experience, I know that you can be searching for a job longer than six months in a recession, so I recommend that you save 10-20k instead of 3-6 months of expenses.

If you live smart and stick to your revised budget for hard times, this can last you up to a year. This makes it easier if you don't want to calculate 3-6 worth of monthly expenses. If you are single, 10k should be fine for you in case of emergencies, but if you have dependents, you want to save higher, around 15-20k.

I can't stress how important it is to have this rainy-day fund. Bad things can, and will, happen, and if you don't plan for them, you are failing to plan, and if you fail to plan, you plan to fail. If you made it this far in the book, you are already in the habit of saving money, because you paid off your student loans and now you have more money in your budget. Go ahead and get used to eliminating monthly bills; there will be plenty of that later on!

STEP 10
INVEST 15-25% OF YOUR INCOME

Finally, we reached my favorite section of this guide: investing! It's finally time to make some money and build our wealth and fortune. I will try to make investing clear, concise, and easy to use. After reading over 25 financial guides and books about investing, I noticed that sometimes they loss their reader by going into the super detail. I want to make sure that one concept is explained thoroughly before we begin with the actual investing talk and that is the power of compounding interest and portfolio diversification.

Compounding interest is the best friend of a person who is on the path to financial freedom and independence. Compounding interest is the concept that all interest you make on an investment will also start compounding and start making you money as well. For example, let's say you have 100k and you have a 10% compounding interest rate per year. After year 1 of this compounding interest rate, you will have 110k. Starting from year two after another year of compounding interest, you will take the 110k from the previous year and multiply that by 10% interest for this year (110k*.10= 121k). Using the principal of Compounding Interest, you earned an extra one grand from the interest on the interest that you earned from year one.

Let's look at an example for simple interest and compare it to our previous example of compounding interest. Simple Interest is where you are only receiving interest on the original principal. Let's take our last example and let's say you have 100k and you have a 10% simple interest rate per year. After year 1, you have 110k. Starting from year two, since it's simple interest, you will only take the principal amount of 100k and multiply that by the simple interest rate, so it will be 100k*.10= 110+10k from the year before to equal 120k instead.

Now that you see the power of compound interest, all our investments will try and incorporate this fact. Below is an example of compounding interest versus simple interest over a long period of time:

Interest Rate	10% per annum	
	Simple Interest earned	Compound Interest earned
Initial deposit	$10,000	$10,000
Year 1	$1,000	$1,000
Year 2	$1,000	$1,100
Year 3	$1,000	$1,210
Year 4	$1,000	$1,331
Year 5	$1,000	$1,464.10
Year 6	$1,000	$1,610.51
Year 7	$1,000	$1,771.56
Year 8	$1,000	$1,948.72
Year 9	$1,000	$2,143.59
Year 10	$1,000	$2,357.95
Total Interest earned	$10,000	$15,937

Portfolio diversification is the realization of the phrase, "Don't put all your eggs into one basket". This phrase is especially true when it comes to investing. You don't have to lose all your money if one stock goes bad or the stock market disappears or the real estate market crashes. In our portfolio, we will have diversification, for example, we will have precious metals in our portfolio; instead of just buying gold, we will buy gold and silver. This will allow your portfolio to do well and not be devastated under any situation that may arise.

Another concept that we will be implementing is Dollar Cost Averaging. Dollar cost Averaging is instead of investing all of your money at a certain price level or percentage, it means to spread out your buying of that particular asset over time as the price decreases. This will allow you to get more of a particular asset, which in return means that you will make more money and bring you closer to financial freedom.

It's imperative that I talk about a couple of concepts before delving deeper in the investment discussion. I want to briefly discuss the concept of net worth, what passive income is, and the different types and streams of passive income. Understanding this concept will make it easier to understand why investing is important and help formulate a mind that is thinking about money and finances correctly. The two most important numbers when it comes to wealth, finances, and being financially independent and free, are net worth and net passive income. The reason why these are the two most important numbers is that these two concepts truly indicate a person's true wealth.

For example, if you were to Google how rich or wealthy someone is, how is their wealth evaluated? I would bet 100 dollars that the number that is displayed is their net worth. If you are wondering what your net worth is or how to calculate it, take the monetary value of all your assets including business, investments, real estate, cars, and etc. – and minus any debt that you have including student debt, mortgages, and personal debts.

The link below includes a net worth calculator to making calculating this easier: https://www.nerdwallet.com/blog/finance/net-worth-calculator/. If your net worth is negative or extremely low, I promise you by the end of reading and following the steps of this book, you will have at least 1-10-million-dollar net worth.

Let's look at someone that has 10 million dollars in assets, but 11 million in debt. This person in this example may appear to be rich, but in reality, that person has a net worth of -1 million dollars. If you're reading this, what if I told you that you could realistically reach a net worth of 5-10 million? I swear to you that it is not only possible, but also almost a guarantee if you follow the steps in this guide religiously and you start early enough. Obtaining a net worth of 5 million would easily put you in the top 5%

of the wealthiest people in the United States. If you're curious where you stack up with your net worth, I'll provide a table below that provides a range of net worth and its correlated net worth percentile.

Net Worth Percentile	Net Worth
10.0%	-$962.66
20.0%	$4,798.06
30.0%	$18,753.84
40.0%	$49,132.21
50.0%	$97,225.55
60.0%	$169,550.64
70.0%	$279,594.27
80.0%	$499,263.50
90.0%	$1,182,390.36
95.0%	$2,377,985.22
99.0%	$10,374,030.10

Let's discuss the main driving force that will help us reach financial independence and financial freedom. I will begin by giving you two definitions of what passive income is: the technical definition and my revised practical definition.

The technical definition for passive income is below:

Passive income is earnings derived from a rental property, limited partnership, or other enterprise in which a person is not actively involved. As with active income, passive income is usually taxable. However, it is often treated differently by the Internal Revenue Service (IRS).

My revised definition is below:

Passive income is any monthly income stream or revenue that requires less than a single day of work within a month. The reason why I have provided my own definition is because some passive income streams will require a couple hours' worth of work a month but is still essentially completely passive. Unfortunately, very few streams of income are what I would consider truly passive.

Many passive income streams either require a shit ton of long period of upfront work or a hell of a lot of initial capital. For example, if you write a book, all residual sales from the book would be considered passive income, but it requires a ton of upfront work to write, publish, and advertise for your book to get those sales. I will go into more depth about different forms of passive income streams, and which ones we will be implementing for this guide. You can generate passive income with music, business, and content creation, but once again there is a huge upfront cost of time and resources to get to the point where these are generating passive income. The power of passive income allows you to not have to worry about money, work a job, and allows you to master money and most importantly have your money work for you instead of you working for your money.

Now that I have gone on my mini rant about some of the challenges that may be involved with creating passive income streams, I will define some of the different types of passive income and why it is important to have as many different streams of passive incomes as humanly possible. Most millionaires have seven streams of incomes; the reason why they typically have these is due to the concept of portfolio diversification. They accomplish this by producing different streams of passive and active income.

Let me briefly discuss what active income is. It is where you make a direct trade of your time for money, and an example of this would be a 9-5 corporate job. One of the goals of this book is to completely reduce the need of an active income to survive and pay our monthly expenses.

Another very important reason to strive to have at least seven different streams of income is that you'll have a varied tax rate on each of the different streams of income, which essentially means that you will lower your tax burden.

Below is a bullet point list of each of these seven streams of income accompanied by a brief description:

1. **Earned Income**

This income is generated from working a corporate job. This typically is your highest taxed source of income. Taxes in this section can reach up to 40% of your total pay (Active Income).

2. **Profit Income**

This income is generated by selling products for more than you bought or made them for. This is where any of your entrepreneurial adventures would fall under. This can be a source of active or passive income. If you have a side hustle, this would be considered active, because you're trading your additional time for money. If you own a business where you are completely hands off and another person or entity is running your business, that would be considered passive income. Side hustles are taxed at the same rate as earned income which can reach up to 40%. If you have a business, the effective tax rate can be much lower because of the many tax incentives that the government provides to small business (Active or Passive).

3. **Interest Income**

This income is generated by interest on money that you lend to a bank, person, or business. If you're lending money to a bank account, it would be in the form of a savings account, money market account, checking account, or a bank bond. If you're lending money to the Federal Reserve, that would be considered a U.S Treasury. If you're lending money to a business, then you would receive your interest in the form of a corporate bond. If you are acting as a bank and lending to a plethora of people, that would be considered Peer to Peer Lending (Passive Income).

4. Dividend Income

This income is generated by owning dividend stocks, and with dividend stocks, when the company makes money, you get a portion of the total revenue proportioned to your stake of the company on a consistent time basis. This time basis can range from weekly, daily, monthly, quarterly, or annually. Taxes in this can vary greatly from 0% to 20% taxes (Passive Income).

5. Rental Income

This income is generated by renting something to another vendor or user; this typically manifests itself in the form of renting out houses or commercial location to businesses. A vast majority of our passive income will be generated in this area (Passive Income).

6. Residual and Royalty Income

This income is generated whenever someone uses your idea, inventions, strategies, or intellectual property that you have a patent on. Some example includes: books, music, inventions, concepts, and business strategies (Passive Income).

7. Capital Gains

This income is generated when you sell an asset for more than what you originally bought it for. Taxes in this section are considerably lower than compared to earned income. Tax rates can go from 0% to 20%. It can be 0% if you sell a house and reinvest the money you made if you buy another house, we will talk about this part later (Passive Income).

Now that we discussed the different types of passive income streams, the plan is to invest 15-25% of your gross income, this means before taxes, so if you make 70k before taxes, we are going to at least invest 10.5k per year. I recommend investing as close to 25% as possible. If you are in your twenties or thirties and you invest now into the below portfolio allocation, I guarantee you that you will be a multi-millionaire by age 65.

Before I give you what percentages and where you're going to invest your money, I want to restate the concept of portfolio diversification and the importance of it. The concept of portfolio diversification is spreading out your assets across a variety of investments to keep you safe from any potential scenario that can play out. For example, if the stock market crashes and you have 100% of your assets in stocks, you are more than fucked. If you had 50% allocated to stocks and bonds, you at least have 50% of your net worth that is not in shambles.

This final investing allocation is not going to include real estate, because a large portion of our budget will be allocated to this in a later step to set up our real estate train. This will be what generates the majority of our passive income to reach our goals of financial freedom and independence. The below investment portfolio is where you will be putting your 15-25% of your salary for investing purposes. I will explain in depth why I choose these options and why this is the best portfolio allocation for someone who is taking the financial freedom journey.

> **Financial Freedom and Independent Man's Portfolio**
>
> 1. Stocks and Bonds %50
> 2. Real Estate % 25
> 3. Gold/Silver %5
> 4. Cash %5
> 5. Cryptocurrency %5
> 6. Investing in yourself/ business Idea %5
> 7. Angel Investing/P2P lending %5

I believe the above allocation provides excellent portfolio diversification, has a great diversification between low-risk and high-reward options, and prepares you for any economic possible scenario. This above guide is what your portfolio allocation should always look like, and if not adjust the allocation of each asset to match the above portfolio. This is to guarantee that you will not be over or underexposed to any one asset. The allocation above is not what the percentages of the left-over money from our monthly budget will be invested in, because the above allocation includes real estate and our actual investment portfolio where we will invest the 15-25% of our portfolio allocation will not. The majority of the allocation is allocated towards stocks and bonds with 50% because the stock market has a long history, dating over 100 years, of constant growth, which gives a great average return of 11% historically accounting for both bull and bear markets.

The above allocation has 25% of exposure to real estate because it is a fairly low-risk medium-to-high-reward investment opportunity if you are buying non-risky real estate properties. Another reason why we are allocating such a large percentage is because no matter what condition the market is in, people will always need a place to stay. The above portfolio has 5% in precious metals in order to account for any scenario where your government's current monetary system collapses. You're probably wondering why we are planning for something like that. I can tell you that the concept of fiat money, which means any currency that is backed by the economy of the government is not sustainable. The reason why I say this is because nothing is really backing the monetary system and the government can print any amount of new money to enter the economy.

As an example of the above claims, our government system in the United States is currently 17 trillion dollars in debt and instead of decreasing our debt, the U.S is increasing it by spending more money every year. This is not just a situation that is happening in the United States; virtually every government system uses fiat money and is in debt. I might be wrong about the above scenario and I hope that I am, but it doesn't hurt to hedge against it anyway and you will probably make money while in the process of hedging against traditional monetary policies. The above allocation has 5% in cash because you should always have some liquid assets in case of any opportunities that may arise.

The above allocation has 5% in cryptocurrency, and I understand that a lot of people and financial advisors will disagree with this part of the allocation. I will make this part of the allocation optional, meaning that if you plan not to invest in cryptocurrency, increase your allocation to other assets that you see fit to compensate for the lack of cryptocurrency in your allocation. Even though the cryptocurrency part of the allocation is optional, I still believe that cryptocurrency is the future and I will explain later on why I believe that. If you don't like cryptocurrency, I would still advise you to allocate 1% to it. You should always have at least 1% of cryptocurrency to have at least some exposure to it. The next part of the allocation has 5% allocated to investing in yourself, which has the potential to have the biggest return out of all these above investments, because there is no cap on the potential return for this allocation. The Angel Investing/Peer to Peer Lending section of our portfolio allocation is also optional and if you plan to not allocate a percentage of your investment funds into it, allocate it towards other sections of the portfolio allocation that you feel more comfortable investing into.

I am a huge advocate of angel investing and peer to peer lending. I will explain later what angel investing and peer to peer lending is and why I love them as investment options. Let me give you an example of how my leftover money in my monthly budget would be allocated after I pay off my personal and student debts.

I currently have $2650 in my budget leftover after paying my monthly expenses, paying off my debt, saving for a rainy-day fund, and accounting for my 3% annual pay raises and the fact that I no longer have the $300 student loan monthly expense. After putting 6% towards my 401k for my match and paying health insurance, that leaves me with $3000 dollars left over to invest. Let's also assume that I'm currently paying double payments on my starter house payment of $800 to pay it off in 4 years, (I'll talk about this in a later section, so don't worry if this is currently confusing), that leaves me with $1400 dollars left to invest.

Since I'm putting $1600 towards my starter home, we aren't' going to put additional money towards real estate. Therefore, we are not going to allocate any of $1400 in this scenario towards real estate, because the asset allocation will already be covered in a later section of our portfolio allocation. The actual allocation of what percentages we would put the $1400 is below and does not include real estate. I just want to restate that the above allocation portfolio should only be considered for portfolio diversification purposes and not the percentages of what you would invest your leftover money from your monthly expenses. I would suggest using the financial tool of personal capital to keep up with what percent allocation you have to keep it balanced.

Personal Capital is a tool which shows you what percentage of your investment portfolio is allocated to what. This can be achieved by creating an account and linking your financial accounts such as your 401k, etc. You can link your real estate properties or manually enter the value of a particular asset. This makes it extremely easy to keep track of what percentages of your portfolio allocation that you currently have.

A guide to using personal capital for portfolio allocation tracking is below: https://investorjunkie.com/43696/started-personal-capital/.

Link to personal capital is below:

https://www.personalcapital.com/.

I can't recommend Personal Capital enough because it makes it extremely easy to know exactly what your current portfolio allocation is. If you need additional help setting up a personal capital account or setting your portfolio allocation, I highly recommend looking up user guides on YouTube because they are extremely easy to follow.

Actual Allocation Not including our real estate train system

Stocks and Bonds: %67.5

Gold/Silver/Platinum: %6.5

Cash: %6.5

Cryptocurrency: %6.5

Investing in yourself: %6.5

Angel Investing/P2P Lending: %6.5

As you can see from the new portfolio allocation above, I have adjusted the percentage for each allocation by a flat percentage increase to account for 25% of real estate that we are not investing directly into with the money left over from our monthly budget. Let us add an additional condition before we look at the percentages of where we will start investing into. In my scenario, I am going to increase how much we are contributing to my 401k from 6% to 15%, which takes $200 dollars from my investment pool of $1600 dollars and brings it down to $1400 dollars. I also highly recommend doing this as well once you have paid off your debt and have saved for a rainy-day fund.

For our stock and bond allocation, we are going to have a mix between a Roth IRA, which I suggest you do through your 401k

IRA account and for your personal IRA, I suggest having a Traditional IRA. The reason why we want our Roth IRA to be our 401k, if possible, is because we can get around the 5600 maximum that you can put in a Roth IRA by having it be a 401k Roth IRA instead, your maximum contributions instead change to $19,000. The difference between the two is that a traditional IRA is pre-tax dollars, which means it's taken out before taxes are applied, so that means that if you're saving 15% of your checks in a traditional IRA, it might be closer to 10% after taxes. The downside of a traditional IRA is that when you take money out of the traditional IRA, you pay taxes when you take money out of that account. A Roth IRA means you have already paid taxes on that money through your job, but when you take the money out it's not taxed.

It's a good idea to have both a traditional IRA and Roth IRA for the same principles of portfolio diversification that we discussed above. A Roth IRA account is better if you are expecting to be in a higher tax bracket when you are older compared to now, which if you're following this guide you will be. And vice versa for traditional IRA, meaning that it is better if you are in a lower tax bracket when you are older. I don't expect the latter of these scenarios to happen, but it is good to plan for any potential situations that may arise. We have diversification on our portfolio with two different types of IRA stock/bond accounts. There is a catch when it comes to Roth IRA though because the government can't let you get away that easy. The catch is that you can't contribute fully to a Roth IRA or Roth 401k if you make more than the amount of $137,000 if you are single or $203,000 combined salary, if you are married.

The good news is that both you and your wife can have separate Roth IRAs and Roth 401k. The limit for a Roth IRA as of 2019 is 6,000 per year if you plan to have your 401k as a traditional IRA instead of a Roth IRA. If you take this route, the plan is to max the 6,000 limit for bonds and stocks. This falls right around our 50% allocation for our investment funds. The mathematical breakdown for the allocation is $100 allocation from our original 6% to our 401k + $200 allocation from our additional 9% allocation of our 401k + $500 that will go to max out our

Roth IRA or put $6,000 towards a traditional IRA account. This leaves us with $800 dollars left over in our investment fund to allocate to the rest of our portfolio allocation. 6.5% of the initial $1600 dollars investment will be allocated towards precious metals like gold and silver.

I recommend rotating between these two precious metals; this is because they both have a long history of being used as currency and are traditionally a hedge against traditional markets such as the stock market. During a recession, the stock market and the value of the dollar will go down, but the price of precious metals will go up. Let's look at our allocation for cash in our example, 6.5% of our initial $1600 dollars will be dedicated to cash. This cash can be used for a variety of things such as increasing the amount of money in your rainy-day fund, keeping it in your checking account, or waiting for an opportunity to invest in a potential business or during times of economic hardship, which I'll discuss later. Investing opportunities will pop up in life, and if you aren't prepared with some liquid assets, you will not be able to take advantage of the opportunity.

6.5% of our $1600 allocation will be dedicated to cryptocurrency. 6.5% will be dedicated to investing in yourself or a business, and another 6.5% will be allocated to investing in angel investing and/or P2P lending. I will elaborate in detail about cryptocurrency, investing in yourself, and investing in angel investment, and/or P2P lending later. This allocation and portfolio is a great mix of traditional and nontraditional investments of high, medium, and low risk designed to maximum your long time return on your money and to provide portfolio diversification.

My investment strategy and portfolio allocation is not designed to be sexy or get you rich overnight. This is an allocation to get you rich over a long period of time using the concepts of market cycles and compounding interest. I understand that some of you don't like the idea of low risk, medium-return investments and want crazy yearly returns. I am sad to tell you that the majority of people and advertisers that you have seen or talked to are either scammers or part of a Ponzi scheme. There is no such thing as a get-rich-quick scheme and/or getting rich overnight besides the lottery. Even people who you assume get rich overnight have grinded for years on years to get to their current position. This is a portfolio designed to give you the maximum possible return over a long period of time while mitigating risk. This portfolio allocation is designed to make the reader a multi-millionaire over a 20-40-year period.

Any financial advisor or person who is saying that they can make you rich over a short period of time without you putting up a ridiculous amount of upfront money is a scammer or being dishonest. There is no such thing as a get-rich-quick scheme, unless you win the lottery which is a scam anyway because it's essentially a tax on the poor. What I mean by a tax on the poor is that, traditionally, only people in lower income neighborhoods play the lottery. If you were to break down the effective cost of a lottery ticket by dividing the chance of you winning by how much money you could potentially win, most lottery tickets are worth less than 50 cents. Every lottery ticket cost more than 50 cents to buy, therefore making it a scam. Instead of leaving your financial future up to a system where you have a one-in-100 million chance to win, you can, however, become financially free and independent by following the principles of this guide.

STOCKS AND BONDS

Stocks and bonds should always be the main part of any person's investment portfolio, because it's a relatively safe investment over a long period of time that averages 8-11% over a year. It is one of the investments with the longest proven track record of returns. The stock market has been around since 1893 and has averaged a 10-11% return. I recommend that you should always have at least 50% of your investment portfolio in stocks and bonds. Most of your portfolio should be in proven traditional investments such as stocks and bonds, because most investments cannot beat an average return of 10% at as low of a risk factor as the stock market.

The strategy that we will follow when it comes to stocks and bonds is to have two different types of stock/bonds account. These different accounts are traditional IRA and Roth IRA, which have different advantages to each as I have talked about in the previous page to the point of ad nauseam. There are technically three options with a SEP (Simplified Employee Pension) IRA, but a SEP would only apply to you if you are self-employed and have very few or no employees. SEPs are considered as traditional IRA meaning that this IRA is a tax deferred investment vehicle. All the rules that apply to traditional IRAs also apply to SEP IRAS. You can put up to 25% of your annual salary in a SEP IRA every year, which is capped at $56,000. If you have employees, you also must match their IRA for any contributions that you make to your SEP IRA.

There is also no catch-up contribution at age 50+ for SEP IRAs. If you're curious about SEP IRAs and you want to open an account once you become self-employed, there is a link below with more information. I would strongly suggest getting a SEP IRA if you're self-employed with no employees and make more than $80,000 dollars a year in profit,

Because SEP IRAs allow you to contribute more to your IRA than a traditional IRA.

Link for SEP IRA is below:

https://clark.com/personal-finance-credit/what-is-a-sep-ira/

The strategy that we will take to manage these funds will be more of a passive role because we don't personally want to keep following the news about each stock and bond. Trust me when I say that the constant keeping up with individual stocks gets tiring real quick. This is not the only reason as to why we are taking a more passive approach to stock and bond investing; typically, people who individually invest in singular stocks and bonds on average get a return of 2% which is 6-8% lower than a traditional index fund. Not only is it more time consuming to micromanage your stocks and bonds, but also there are chances that you'll get a lower return on your money as well. I'm not saying that you cannot manage your own stocks and bonds, but it's a skill that must be learnt that can take anywhere from 100-1000 hours to get good at. I am under the assumption that you don't have 100-1000 hours to master managing and handling your own stocks and bonds.

The main investment vehicle that we will be incorporating for stocks and bonds is index funds. The reason for this is that they have low management and buying fees and typically average around an 8-10% yearly return for a long-term investing strategy. An index fund is a type of mutual fund with a portfolio constructed to match or track the components of a financial market index, such as the Standard & Poor's 500 Index (S&P 500).

An index mutual fund is said to provide broad market exposure, low operating expenses, and low portfolio turnover. I already know that some of you already have the question as to why we are choosing to invest in index funds instead of mutual funds that don't necessarily follow the S&P 500. Dave Ramsey and other financial advisors have said that they are better than index funds. I will let Warren Buffet explain with his famous quote below my opinion on mutual funds verses index fund:

"My money...is where my mouth is: What I advise here is essentially identical to certain instructions I've laid out in my will. One bequest provides that cash will be delivered to a trustee for my wife's benefit. (I must use cash for individual bequests, because all my Berkshire shares will be fully distributed to certain philanthropic organizations over the ten years following the closing of my estate.) My advice to the trustee could not be simpler: Put 10% of the cash in short-term government bonds and 90% in a very low-cost S&P 500 index fund. (I suggest Vanguard's.) I believe the trust's long-term results from this policy will be superior to those attained by most investors—whether pension funds, institutions or individuals—who employ high-fee managers."

Warren buffet has had many bets with people who claim they can beat the S&P 500 over a ten-year period, and all of them have lost especially when they account for their outrageous management fees. If you're going to actively manage your stocks and manually pick which stocks to buy and keep track of, I highly recommend you read the book, *Intelligent Investor* by Warren Buffet. The book has everything that you will need to pick, monitor, and actively manage your stocks and bonds. The book advises against investing in penny stocks due to their lack of history, volatility, and risk associated with them, and I happen to agree. You can become good at trading penny stocks, but it takes a significant number of hours to become a profitable trader. If you have a desire for an asset with high volatility and extremely high potential upside, we will talk about an asset that has all of this and more later in this chapter.

The *Intelligent Investor* is hands down the best book ever written about buying and managing value stocks. To give you a quick synopsis of what the book talks about, it mainly focuses on buying stocks of companies of products that you actually like and use. This provides a system that requires low maintenance to actively keep up with your stocks. In other words, you will automatically know how good or bad the companies that you are investing in are by liking the product. In this way, you know how the company is doing for good or bad and it'll make it easier to do research, because you already like the product.

Like I stated before, I do not prefer this approach, because it takes time, dedication, and some stress in order to keep up with your stocks and bonds. I want the handling of my stocks and bonds to be as passive as humanly possible, and I have found that getting a robo stock broker is the simplest yet most effective way to invest in stocks and bonds as passively as possible.

A robo or robot stock broker is a computer program that looks at trends, historical and new data, and sentiments in the market to automatically manage your funds to give you the best possible return. There are a couple reasons why I prefer robo stock brokers compared to actual human stock brokers. The first and main reason is that they typically outperform actual human stock brokers, because they use algorithms that have been proven over 100 years to work, and robots don't take into account any emotion during trading and managing funds which can cause a lot of human brokers to make rash decisions. The second reason is that they are typically cheaper and give more customization when it comes to how you handle your assets and rebalance your allocations of stocks and bonds. The third reason as to why I prefer robo advisors to traditional financial advisors is because, they typically have very low or no required starting balance. Most financial advisors require a minimum investment of $100,000 — a balance that may be unattainable upfront for many people. Robo advisors have a much lower requirement, as low as $500.

Another reason that robo advisors are better is that you have 24-hour access to your assets and your allocation, something that may not be available at a typical firm. Unlike most firms, robo advisors are there for you when you need them. If you have an internet connection, you can get the help you need at any time. Hopefully, I have convinced you to, at least, look at a potential robo advisor as an option to manage and handle your assets. The robo advisor I personally use and recommend using is Betterment. The reason why I recommend Betterment compared to its competitors is because it offers no minimum account balance. It has 13.5 billion in assets under management, uses automated tax-loss harvesting, asset rebalancing, and it offers a mix of low-fee stock and bond index funds, and has a risk questionnaire which provides you with a customized, diverse portfolio. Their rate is a 0.25% annual fee which is much lower than traditional stock brokers and considered low even among robo advisors.

I believe that the main selling point of Betterment is their risk questionnaire, which based on the questionnaire customizes a strategy for each person and creates an investing strategy that is best for your financial goals based on your risk tolerance. Betterment's automatic portfolio rebalancing feature is amazing and makes the process of reallocation based on age a lot easier. In essence, this rebalancing feature basically creates a system of reallocation that adjusts your exposure to stocks and bonds. For example,t he younger you are, the more you can handle volatility in the market and Betterment allocates a larger percentage of your holdings into stocks, which have a higher risk and potential higher return compared to bonds. Betterment will allocate your money to riskier stocks and bonds which have a potential of higher upside, and since you're so young, if the market crashes, you still have 20-40 years left to make up for it. As you age towards retirement, your portfolio cannot handle the traditional volatility of a portfolio made up almost primarily of stocks.

In this scenario, the reallocation system will increase the percentage of your portfolio that is allocated to bonds to lower the potential volatility; As you get older, the less risky your portfolio becomes because as you get older or closer to retirement, you don't want a stock crash to take 40% of your stock and bond worth. So it will put most of your worth in bonds which basically has zero vol-atility so your assets are safe from a crash when you get older.

If I convinced you to use betterment, set up a Roth IRA or IRA through the list below with its suggested risk for your age after taking their investing goal questionnaire. Choose the retirement plan so that it accounts for your age. If you're in your twenties, choose general investing.

Link to betterment: https://www.betterment.com/start-investing/?dd_pm=none&dd_pm_cat=brokerage&dd_pm_company=betterment

Examples of Money You Can Accumulate over a Lifetime with Stocks

Following the strategies of this book, I can expect 4.1 million in my 401k by the age of 65 and this isn't considering any future potential promotions that would cause a much larger than 3% annual salary increase. The reason why I put my current age at 25 in the example below is because that is when I expect to pay off my debt, save my emergency fund, and be able to put a 20% down payment on my starter home. As this is the plan that we talked about in the previous chapter, I am using the calculator provided by bankrate, because it's easy to use and conveys its point effectively.

Your total is $4,103,761 after 40 years.

401(k) Employee Savings Plan:

Percent to contribute:	15%
Annual salary:	$72,000
Annual salary increase:	3%
Current age:	25
Age of retirement:	65
Current 401(k) balance:	$20,000
Annual rate of return:	7%
Total employee contributions:	$749,970

401(k) Employer Match:

Employer match:	50%
Employer match ends:	6%
Total employer contributions:	$167,753

Link: https://www.bankrate.com/calculators/retirement/401-k-retirement-calculator.aspx

Use the link above to calculate what your expected 401k worth will be when you plan to retire. Enter the information above: Percent to Contribute, Annual Salary, Annual Salary Increase, Current Age, Age of Retirement, Current 401(k) Balance, Annual Rate of Return, Employer Match, and Employer Match Ends to get your expected 401k worth. Unfortunately, you are required to take money out of this account starting at the age 65 because it's a retirement account and the government wants to get its taxes on the money that was deferred.

Another stipulation is that there is 10% fee on any money that you take out before 59. If you have a traditional 401k, meaning that it is tax deferred, you will have to pay taxes when you take money out of your 401k account. This tax rate will be derived from the amount of your annual income at the time you take money out of the account. This includes any passive income, selling of assets, rental property income, any money generated from a business or a service. The one downside of having a lot of passive income is that you will get taxed at a higher tax rate due to the fact that your annual passive income streams are vast. You can expect a fat 33-40% tax rate on this money, but remember that your money was growing tax-free the entire time that you were saving and investing into the traditional 401k account.

An Example of My Expected Roth IRA Growth When I Retire

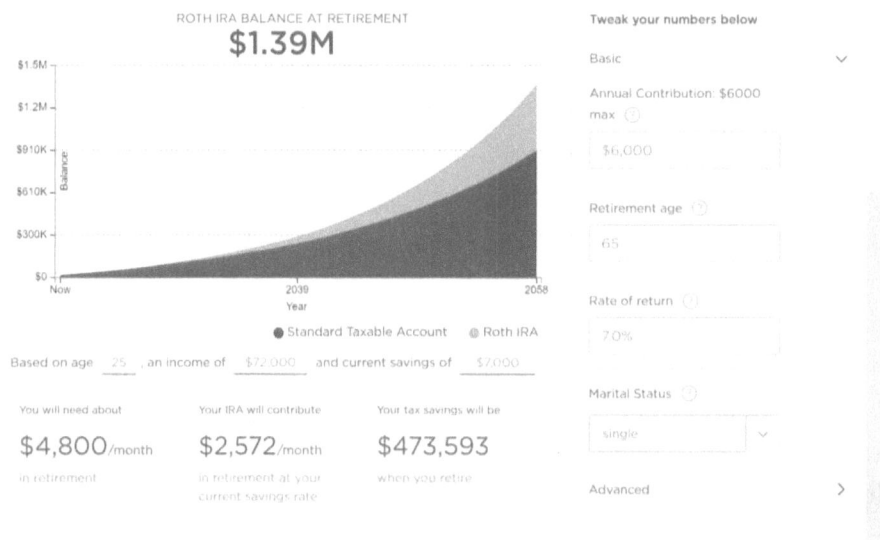

Before we look at the potential growth that you can expect in a Roth IRA Account, remember that you have limits to how much you can make before you can't contribute to your Roth IRA that isn't in a 401k. In 2019, if your adjusted gross income is $203,000 or more as a joint filer or $137,000 or more as a single filer, you're not eligible for a Roth IRA.

Use this link below to estimate how much you will have at retirement for a non-401k retirement account:

https://www.nerdwallet.com/investing/roth-ira-calculator.

Between my Roth IRA and my traditional 401k account, I can expect around $5.5 million dollars in stocks and bonds at the age of 65. Please note that this is an example and I plan to retire way before age 65. This example is to provide you a framework of the power of compounding interest and investing over a long period of time. Please don't worry if you're older than I am in this example, you still will end up with a sizeable amount of money at your retirement age following this strategy.

Some of you are probably wondering why I don't want to work till age 65! This might be controversial, but I recommend that you work till the age of 65, because I believe people should never really stop working completely. I believe people should retire from the job that they aren't passionate about once they reach financial independence/freedom. People should work for themselves and do what they love to do after they become financially independent. If you're in a similar situation to mine, you will have around 5.5 million dollars at the time of your retirement and this is just one portion of your investing portfolio; there are five more sections to go! This was also considering a more conservative return of 7% compared to the historical 10% market the stock market traditionally gives.

Before we move on to the next section of the investing strategy, I want to give an example and a resource to calculate if you should get a traditional 401k or a Roth 401k. I understand that it may not be an easy decision and wanted to provide some visibility into the issue. The below link provides a straight comparison of a traditional 401k and a Roth IRA: https://www.calcxml.com/calculators/ret10?skn=#results

Results

Based on the assumptions you provided, your $10,000 annual contribution for 40 years could provide as much as $213,723 per year ($17,810 per month) for your anticipated 20 year distribution period.

* Actual contribution levels to non-deductible accounts have been reduced to reflect the effects of making after-tax contributions.

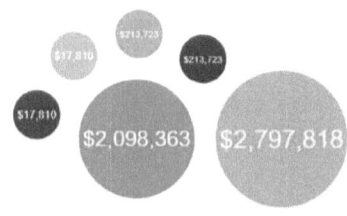

■ Account value at retirement - Roth 401(k)   ■ Account value at retirement - 401(k)
■ After-tax annual income - Roth 401(k)   ■ After-tax annual income - 401(k)
■ After-tax monthly income - Roth 401(k)   ■ After-tax monthly income - 401(k)

The above results show the monetary value of the traditional 401k and a Roth IRA. As you can see, there is about 700,000 dollars more in the traditional Roth IRA compared to the Roth IRA, because it was able to grow tax deferred compared to the Roth IRA.

Summary Table

	401(k) Analysis	
Accumulation Phase	Roth 401(k) (Non-Deductible)	401(k) (Deductible)
Annual contribution (before tax)	$10,000	$10,000
Adjustment for taxable contributions*	-2,500	-0
Total annual contribution (after tax)	$7,500	$10,000
Interest rate (accumulation phase)	8%	8%
Term (accumulation phase)	40	40
Account value at retirement	**$2,098,363**	**$2,797,818**
Distribution Phase	Roth 401(k) (Non-Deductible)	401(k) (Deductible)
Account value at retirement	$2,098,363	$2,797,818
Term (distribution phase)	20	20
Interest rate (distribution phase)	8%	8%
Annual income before taxes	$213,723	$284,964
Annual income tax	$0	$71,241
After-tax annual income	$213,723	$213,723
After-tax monthly income	$17,810	$17,810

The table above shows a summary of the contributions made to the traditional 401k and the Roth IRA accounting for taxes. You can see that after the marginal tax rate of 25%, we are only contributing $7500 to the Roth 401k of the originally $10000 planned. The Roth IRA shows its worth when you don't have to pay taxes on the money when you take it out. You can see that you will have to pay $71,241 in taxes when you take money out of the traditional tax rate.

In this example, you can see that the money that you receive after calculating everything is $17,810 for both the traditional 401k and the Roth 401k per month. Even though the amount of money that you would receive from both the traditional 401k and the Roth IRA is essentially the same in this example, the Roth IRA is a better option because this example doesn't incorporate the fact that you will have a higher tax rate when you retire than the one provided in this example as well as the other passive income that you will have coming in.

GOLD/SILVER

Let us begin by talking about buying precious metals by stating that this is our main investment hedge against the stock and bond market and government financial systems. The reason why we need a hedge is due to the sad reality that the financial systems created by government systems can't always be trusted, and you should hedge against them. It's apparent that if you're reading this guide, you can probably tell that I am not the biggest fan of banks, governments, or their financial systems. One of the main reasons is that their greed caused the 2008 market crash.

The financial crisis was primarily caused by deregulation in the financial industry that permitted banks to engage in hedge fund trading with derivatives. Banks then demanded more mortgages to support the profitable sale of these derivatives. They created interest-only loans that became affordable to subprime borrowers. In 2004, the Federal Reserve raised the fed funds rate just as the interest rates on these new mortgages reset. Housing prices started falling as supply outpaced demand. That trapped homeowners who couldn't afford the payments but couldn't sell their house. When the values of the derivatives crumbled, banks stopped lending to each other and that created the financial crisis that led to the Great Recession.

The United States is currently 17 trillion dollars in debt with no current plan to reduce or pay off this debt. The United States government spends more money annually than they have coming in. The Federal Reserve prints more and more money that is not backed by anything but the economy of the United States government. This system is not sustainable, and it will collapse eventually. It might take three hundred years, but it will eventually collapse. We will plan for the worst possible scenario, because if you fail to plan, you plan to fail. Precious metals are a great hedge against this, because they are one of the most stable forms of currencies in history, if not the most stable.

If you're not familiar with the term "hedge," a hedge is defined as a way of protecting oneself against financial loss or other adverse circumstances. The stock market and the price of precious metals have an inverse return model, which means when stock prices typically go up, gold prices go down and when stock prices go down, gold prices go up. The last statement only applies to recessions and market corrections, but does not apply to economic depressions. Not only gold prices, prices of just about everything go down during an economic depression, but economic depressions are extremely rare and on average you would experience one during your lifetime. Gold is not technically a 100% hedge against the stock market, but it's the best option that we have given the circumstances of economic downtimes.

In our portfolio allocation for precious metals, we are going to accumulate both gold and silver. The reason why we aren't just buying gold and we are buying silver is because even though it is a hedge against traditional markets, we still want our money allocated towards precious metals to grow. If you adjust the price of gold for inflation over the last thousand years, it has not gone up in price significantly, if at all, and as far as investments go, it's a pretty low yield one. As of 2019, I am expecting a 30-40% correction in the United States stock market soon. This could provide a lucrative opportunity to own gold as its price could skyrocket, but we aren't counting on that.

Silver is a significantly more volatile asset compared to gold but has a much higher potential return on your investment as well. The gold-to-silver ratio, which is a typical indicator of indicating if the price of gold or silver is underpriced compared to the vice versa asset, is at a 28-year high for silver at an ounce ratio for 93 to 1.This means that silver is at its most undervalued state in 28 years compared to gold as of writing this guide in 2019. When the ratio of gold to silver rises about 80 to 1, that is typically an indicator that silver is underpriced and gold is overpriced, and vice versa. When the ratio drops below 40 to 1, that typically means that silver is overpriced and gold is underpriced.

As I just stated in the last statement, a gold-to-silver ratio of 93 to 1 either means that silver is significantly undervalued, or gold is significantly overvalued and it is extremely more probable that silver will, at least, double from $15 dollars to $30 an ounce due to the fact that silver has experienced prices of $100 dollars in the past, instead of the price of an ounce of gold going from $1400 to $700.

The graph of the last 100-year historical gold to silver ratio is below as an example of the previous statement:

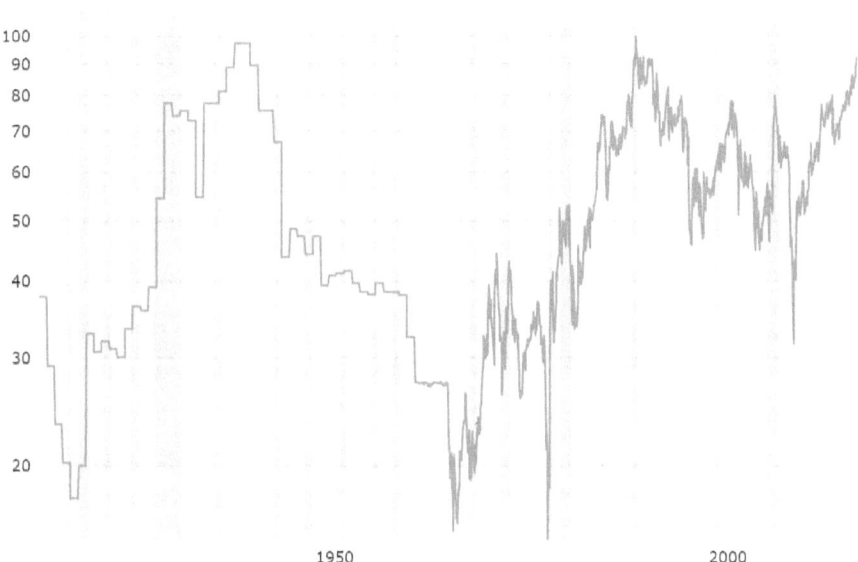

100-Year Historical Data of Gold-Silver Ratio

As of the time of writing this guide in 2019, my plan when it comes to silver is to sell 50% of my holdings at the price point at $100 dollars per troy ounce and buy more gold or the ratio of gold-to-silver returns to a historical average of 40 ounces of silver compared to 1 ounce of gold. This is currently my exit strategy for silver due to the fact that the all-time high price for silver is $200 dollars, so I don't think it's beyond the realm of comprehension for it to reach $100 dollars again during its major price movement up. Silver, when it starts to trend upwards, tends to exponentially move in a short period of time. Therefore, you should never try to time the price of silver and you should dollar cost in like every other asset that we will invest in. Having our precious metals allocation consist of both gold and silver allows us to potentially make some substantial returns while we hedge against traditional markets.

You should have a buying strategy when it comes to buying precious metals because you can lose some value during the buying process if done incorrectly. Our buying strategy will be every month; we will alternate between buying gold and silver and we will only ever buy physical gold and silver and not gold or silver-based ETF. If you are unaware of what an ETF is, it is a publicly Exchanged Traded Fund. In layman's terms, a physically backed silver or gold ETF is essentially a piece of paper that states you own the gold or silver that it is referring to. The issue with gold and silver-based ETFs is that these ETFs are referring to two to three times the amount of gold and silver that is thought to be in circulation. Only buy gold and silver in .9999 24k pure gold or pure silver bars.

You technically can potentially get a better dollar to precious metal ratio by buying certain gold and silver coins, but that requires some expertise and it may make it harder to sell when you want to convert back to your currency. We will just stick to buying .9999 pure gold or silver bars for simplicity's sake. Never buy gold or silver jewelry as an investment because it possibly can lose 10-20% of its value when you try to sell it back if you don't know what you are doing when buying for investments. The reason why it loses its value is because when these sellers typically try to melt your jewelry into bar form, some gold and silver will be lost in the process of converting the jewelry to the form of gold and silver bars. Another reason why buying jewelry as an investment is not a good idea is that the purity of the jewelry can vastly impact your potential return on your investment.

I recommend buying gold and silver from eBay and Amazon, but only buy from this list of sellers: PinehurstCoins, CreditSuisse, Scottsdale, International trade bullion, PAMP, THE PRTH MINT AUSTRSALIA, ARGOR_HERAEUS, RMC REPUBLIC and never pay above 1-2% above spot; this means 1-2% above the market price for that weight you are buying. I recommend buying gold in troy ounces that are in their original package with the certification in the package to verify that it is .9999 mint gold. I recommend buying silver in 100-ounce increments because it makes it easier to store and stack. If you're going to store gold and silver in your house, don't tell anyone for your own safety.

I also recommend that you always have three layers of visibility protection against theft. What I mean by visibility protection is that a thief would have to move or adjust three objects to get to your silver or gold. For example, have a coffee table on top of a rug and have a safe in a compartment in the floor. This will almost assuredly protect you against theft even if someone finds out that you store precious metals in your house.

If you're interested in how to properly store your gold and silver, the YouTube link below goes into great detail about how to protect your precious metals from theft:
https://www.youtube.com/watch?v=SXFLZub7DaU.

CASH

Before we begin looking at what we are allocating our cash for in our portfolio allocation, let me begin by explaining why we are allocating a portion of our investment allocation towards cash. You're probably wondering why you need more cash. I already stated in a previous chapter that owning a lot of cash is a terrible investment. While it is true that you actively lose 1-3% of your cash worth due to inflation every year, I don't want to understate and undersell the power of having some liquid assets to invest at opportune times. One example of where you would want some liquid assets to invest is: if one of your friends is currently inventing some new technology that has the potential to impact the world and would give you 5% of the company for 5k. If you didn't have enough liquid assets to do it, you just missed out on a once-in-a-lifetime opportunity.

I just want to be clear that this cash that we are actively allocating a percent of our investing allocation towards is different from the 2-5k in your checking account for emergencies and the 10-20k for your rainy-day fund in your money market or savings accounts. This money is going to be used primarily used for investing opportunities that may arise during your lifetime; I will go into more detail about some of these possible scenarios later.

Another use for this money could be as a larger rainy-day fund, and from working with various people, I've come to terms that some people like to have large sums of cash in reserve for their own peace of mind and sanity. If you're wondering what type of cash reserve that would be available to you after following this strategy, using myself as an example, I should have around $150,000 worth of cash in reserve at around age 65. Another reason why we have 6.5% allocated for cash in our investment portfolio is for any corrections, bear markets, and recessions, or black swan events in the stock market. These provide great opportunities to make good safe returns over a period of a couple of years.

Just to give you a brief history of the stock market, since 1926 to today, what percentage of the market has been in the positive if you had to guess? It breaks down to a staggering 74% positive and 26% negative. This equates to on average for every nine years of economic growth in the stock market, there is three years of economic decline. As of the time of writing this book, we are nearing 10 years of economic growth. As a logical person, you know that we will eventually have to start going down according to the historical data of the stock market. Thankfully, we have the foresight to be able to plan for this and make a ton of money off this event.

Let's briefly talk about the different types of ways markets can down. An economic depression lasts two years and GDP decreases by 10%, an economic recession is a six months; decline, and a correction is typically a short period of time when the market goes down around 11-13% on average. A black swan event is a geographical event that cannot be planned for such as a 9/11 attack or an assassination of a country's president. We will not plan for a depression, recession, correction, or black swan. We will plan for a bear market, and a bear market can be a combination of all the above different types of down-market terms. Typically, in a bear market, the market corrects 30% from its market cycle high on average. You're probably thinking that since more than 50% of our investing portfolio is already allocated towards stocks, why are we putting more money into stocks?

Yes, I understand that we already have a section dedicated to stocks, but we can briefly have a higher allocation to stocks and bonds if that means we can increase our wealth significantly in 3-5 years. The money that we will putting into this particular stock allocation is different from the 50% stock allocation that we talked about before because we are going to cost average into the market after the market has declined significantly instead of dollar cost averaging, regardless of the price. We already have a section of our inventing allocation that is set to invest every day, regardless of what the market is doing and that is typically what you should do to prevent yourself from being too cautious or too optimistic. You should never try to time the exact bottom of a bear market because you will drive yourself insane and more than likely wait too long or get in way too early. What we will do instead is dollar cost averaging into the market during a bear market where it has declined by 30% or more. We will enter the market at 30% and below, because that historically has been the bottom for most bear markets.

Some of you are probably saying that we will miss the bottom if that is the historical bottom, and you may be right, but we are not in a rush to enter the market and we can let our cash reserve grow for another opportunity if it never reaches a 30% decline.

If you're interested in the data that went into calculating the theoretical average bottom of bear markets starting from 1956 to now, I have provided a table of past bear markets below:

History of Bear and Bull Markets Starting from 1956

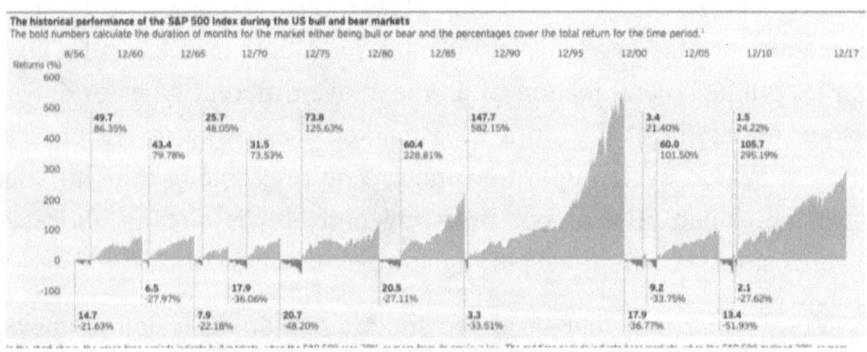

The current plan for our dollar cost averaging is to wait for the stock market to decline by 30%, then put 50% of our cash reserves into a high-yield dividend stock investing account. After every 5% additional decline in the market, we will allocate another 15% of our cash reserves to buy more stock for our investing stock account. Please don't worry and think that this investment account is going to be high maintenance and that you will have to look at and keep up with individual stocks all day to do this. We will talk in detail about a strategy that turns this high-yield dividend stock investing account into a low maintenance account that requires little to no upkeep. This strategy will help us lower our initial entry price point for which we have effectively bought stocks, and a lower entry price point essentially means more stocks and bonds that you have bought.

Dollar cost averaging is the best possible strategy to enter any market, due to the fact that if you dollar cost average, it prevents you from buying into the market at too high of a price when you think the market has finished crashing or has bottomed. An important fact to know is that markets cycles have similarities, but markets are unpredictable on exactly how high or low they can go, and they have the potential to go way higher or way lower than you can ever imagine. For example, during the great recession starting from the 2008 housing and banking crisis, the market crashed by a staggering 54%, and absolutely no one predicted that. The reason why we are entering the market around 30% is because that has been the mean low of the past bear markets. The stock market has reached all-time highs once again and has been on a 10-year bull market, which means it's been increasing for the past 10 years and I expect at least a 30% correction from the all-time highs that we are experiencing late in 2019.

In order to make sure that this high-yield dividend investing portfolio remains low maintenance, I highly recommend creating a M1 finance account. It's totally free and makes it super easy to invest and follow other successful investors' portfolios for free! This type of tool is typically only for institutional investors that have millions or billions of dollars to invest, but due to technological advances and the fact that a lot more everyday people are starting to invest, we now have access to finance tools such as M1 finance.

Here is a link to the M1 finance website: https://www.m1finance.com/.

If you are interested, I currently plan to invest 25k into a portfolio created by Joseph Carlson as of 2019 once the market declines by 30%, because he is a very intelligent guy that manages and holds a high-dividend investing portfolio. As of writing this book, he has grown a 25k account into 42k over a 6-month period.

Here is a link to Joseph Carlson's portfolio: https://urlzs.com/U45YH

If for some reason you don't like Joseph Carlson's portfolio allocation and/or you want to try a different allocation, there are literally thousands of portfolios that you can follow on M1 Finance. If possible, I would try and grow this high-yield stock dividend account to around 25k dollars because the dividend returns will be big enough to buy whole shares of companies which will decrease the time it will take to increase your money through dividends. A dividend is the equivalent of a company paying you for holding their stock, which is more importantly equivalent to a source of passive income. Another reason that I like high-yield dividend stocks for passive income is that, believe it or not, traditionally dividend stocks outperform index funds by a 1 or 2%. In our actual stocks and bonds allocation, 50% of our total investing portfolio is all index funds. This provides us exposure to both index funds and high-yield dividend stocks, which provides us more diversification in our stocks and bonds allocation.

As you are aware, in this secondary stock account, we will invest only in high-yield dividend stocks because it provides a passive income stream that is less reliant on the current market cycle and structure.

If you're interested in examples or data that show how dividend stocks outperform index funds, here is a link: https://www.thebalance.com/why-dividend-stocks-outperform-non-dividend-stocks-357353.

If you have been reading this book up to this point, you know that we love passive income, which is why we are choosing a high-dividend investing strategy compared to stocks that don't give a dividend. We will reinvest all dividends from this portfolio back into buying more stock so that the investment account can grow quicker and give you more and more passive income every year. This will decrease the time it takes you to become financially free and financially independent. Once you decide to retire, you can continue to let this account and take the typical 3-4% dividend of passive income.

Below is a link that provides you a calculator to see how much passive income you can generate from an initial investment of 25,000 dollars:

https://www.investopedia.com/calculator/dvcal.aspx.

I'll use myself to provide you an example of the type of passive income you could possibly receive from high-yield dividend stocks. Below is the data I entered to generate the table that has all the numbers for the potential return of this investment account.

Initial Investment	25000
Monthly Additional Investment	200
Assumed Dividend Growth Rate	5 %
Assumed Dividend Yield	3.5 %
Assumed Reinvestment Duration	20 years
Assumed Inflation Rate	4.10 %
Assumed Growth Rate of Share Price	6 %
Current Age	25

Calculate

Table that Shows the Potential Long-Term Return for an High-Yield Dividend Account

Future Age	Year	Year #	Actual Annual Dividend Paid	Inflation Adjusted Dividend Paid in today's $	Year-End Actual Portfolio Value	Year-End Inflation Adjusted Portfolio Value in today's $
25	2019	1	$0.00	$0.00	$27,049.79	$27,049.79
26	2020	2	$0.00	$0.00	$30,033.70	$30,033.70
27	2021	3	$0.00	$0.00	$32,903.25	$32,903.25
28	2022	4	$0.00	$0.00	$36,035.81	$36,035.81
29	2023	5	$0.00	$0.00	$39,454.48	$39,454.48
30	2024	6	$0.00	$0.00	$43,184.35	$43,184.35
31	2025	7	$0.00	$0.00	$47,252.58	$47,252.58
32	2026	8	$0.00	$0.00	$51,688.64	$51,688.64
33	2027	9	$0.00	$0.00	$56,524.44	$56,524.44
34	2028	10	$0.00	$0.00	$61,794.56	$61,794.56
35	2029	11	$0.00	$0.00	$67,536.45	$67,536.45
36	2030	12	$0.00	$0.00	$73,790.65	$73,790.65
37	2031	13	$0.00	$0.00	$80,601.07	$80,601.07
38	2032	14	$0.00	$0.00	$88,015.22	$88,015.22
39	2033	15	$0.00	$0.00	$96,084.51	$96,084.51
40	2034	16	$0.00	$0.00	$104,864.56	$104,864.56
41	2035	17	$0.00	$0.00	$114,415.55	$114,415.55
42	2036	18	$0.00	$0.00	$124,802.52	$124,802.52
43	2037	19	$0.00	$0.00	$136,095.83	$136,095.83
44	2038	20	$0.00	$0.00	$148,371.50	$148,371.50
45	2039	21	$4,296.23	$4,296.23	$157,273.79	$157,273.79
46	2040	22	$4,511.04	$4,511.04	$166,710.21	$166,710.21
47	2041	23	$4,736.59	$4,736.59	$176,712.83	$176,712.83
48	2042	24	$4,973.42	$4,973.42	$187,315.60	$187,315.60
49	2043	25	$5,222.09	$5,222.09	$198,554.53	$198,554.53
50	2044	26	$5,483.20	$5,483.20	$210,467.80	$210,467.80
51	2045	27	$5,757.35	$5,757.35	$223,095.87	$223,095.87

52	2046	28	$6,045.22	$6,045.22	$236,481.62	$236,481.62
53	2047	29	$6,347.48	$6,347.48	$250,670.52	$250,670.52
54	2048	30	$6,664.86	$6,664.86	$265,710.75	$265,710.75
55	2049	31	$6,998.10	$6,998.10	$281,653.40	$281,653.40
56	2050	32	$7,348.01	$7,348.01	$298,552.60	$298,552.60
57	2051	33	$7,715.41	$7,715.41	$316,465.76	$316,465.76
58	2052	34	$8,101.18	$8,101.18	$335,453.70	$335,453.70
59	2053	35	$8,506.24	$8,506.24	$355,580.93	$355,580.93
60	2054	36	$8,931.55	$8,931.55	$376,915.78	$376,915.78
61	2055	37	$9,378.12	$9,378.12	$399,530.73	$399,530.73
62	2056	38	$9,847.03	$9,847.03	$423,502.57	$423,502.57
63	2057	39	$10,339.38	$10,339.38	$448,912.73	$448,912.73
64	2058	40	$10,856.35	$10,856.35	$475,847.49	$475,847.49
65	2059	41	$11,399.17	$11,399.17	$504,398.34	$504,398.34
66	2060	42	$11,969.13	$11,969.13	$534,662.24	$534,662.24
67	2061	43	$12,567.58	$12,567.58	$566,741.97	$566,741.97
68	2062	44	$13,195.96	$13,195.96	$600,746.49	$600,746.49
69	2063	45	$13,855.76	$13,855.76	$636,791.28	$636,791.28
70	2064	46	$14,548.55	$14,548.55	$674,998.76	$674,998.76
71	2065	47	$15,275.98	$15,275.98	$715,498.68	$715,498.68
72	2066	48	$16,039.78	$16,039.78	$758,428.61	$758,428.61
73	2067	49	$16,841.76	$16,841.76	$803,934.32	$803,934.32
74	2068	50	$17,683.85	$17,683.85	$852,170.38	$852,170.38

CRYPTOCURRENCY

Now, it's time to talk about my favorite section of this whole book, which is cryptocurrency. Where do I even begin with cryptocurrency? I'll start by explaining the concept behind cryptocurrency and what exactly it is. A cryptocurrency is a digital asset designed to work as a medium of exchange that uses strong cryptography to secure financial transactions, control the creation of additional units, and verify the transfer of assets. It uses technology called blockchain, which is a digital ledger that basically allows you to make anonymous transactions that are not changeable and are verified by other users on the network. This, in combination with cryptography, is a concept to keep transactions safe, unchangeable, and encoded and makes for an awesome payment solution.

There has always been a huge issue with digital cash that has been solved with the rise of cryptocurrency. The huge issue with digital cash is the double spend problem, which is the concept that while a transaction is pending or waiting to be confirmed, another transaction with the same allocated money for the first transaction can be created. This causes huge issues within banking and credit cards, which is why they must manually validate each transaction and why transactions through the traditional financial systems can take days or even weeks to validate and approve. Cryptocurrency solves this issue with the combination of cryptography and blockchain.

I understand that you are probably thoroughly confused after reading all that technical jargon. This is called the common man's guide to investing, so I'm going to simplify it into an understandable statement. In layman's term, it's essentially the perfect form of currency, because it's scarce with a maximum of only 21 million supply, almost infinitely divisible, durable, programmable, easily transferable, irreversible, decentralized, and secure. Decentralized means that not one single entity controls bitcoin because of the nodes that validate the system and make it safe. In other words, there are thousands, if not tens of thousands, of people who are validating transactions and keeping the bitcoin network up. It's so secure and decentralized; in fact, if every government system in the world tried to stop bitcoin, they literally would be powerless to do so.

As long as there is one node still active, bitcoin would keep running. If the government started trying to close bitcoin nodes, for every one node that they would close, two more nodes would pop up to continue to secure the network. Gold and silver are a great hedge against traditional financial systems and governments, but it cannot compete with the potential hedge against traditional financial systems and governments that cryptocurrency provides. This is because cryptocurrency is a truly no-correlated asset; when it comes to it, cryptocurrency marches to the sound of its own flute. This creates the perfect hedge to both good and bad times when it comes to the stock market and the global economy.

Below is a chart that visualizes the advantages that cryptocurrency has over fiat currency or commodities such as gold and silver:

Chart comparing Gold vs Fiat vs Crypto Traits of Money

Traits of Money	Gold	Fiat (US Dollar)	Crypto (Bitcoin)
Fungible (Interchangeable)	High	High	High
Non-Consumable	High	High	High
Portability	Moderate	High	High
Durable	High	Moderate	High
Highly Divisible	Moderate	Moderate	High
Secure (Cannot be counterfeited)	Moderate	Moderate	High
Easily Transactable	Low	High	High
Scarce (Predictable Supply)	Moderate	Low	High

Why do I love cryptocurrency so much? There're so many different reasons that if I list them all, this section would be 100 pages and I promised to make this guide as short and concise as humanly possibly while still hitting all of the important parts. The first and one of the main reasons is the programmable scarcity that bitcoin provides with its maximum amount of 21 million. You are probably making the argument about the scarcity of gold, and while it is true that we can't make more gold, we mine more and more gold each year, so it still has a pseudo inflation rate until we mine all of it up, which will take thousands of years.

Gold does have scarcity, because there is only so much gold in our earth crust. The difference between programmable and perceived scarcity is that with perceived scarcity, our assumption could always be wrong. For example, let's say that a gold asteroid hits earth tomorrow which is extremely unlikely, but for argument sake, the price of gold would plummet because it would be readily available to everyone and gold would not be perceived as scarce anymore.

Bitcoin provides the world with a never–seen-before true deflationary currency or asset. On top of that, it's assumed that around 3 million bitcoins are already lost, so it makes bitcoin even more scarce because the actual maximum supply is closer to 18 million bitcoins instead of 21 million. To put in perspective just how scarce of a commodity bitcoin is, there are 36 million millionaires in the world. This means if every millionaire wanted to buy some bitcoin and the allocation was divided evenly, which it isn't and won't be, the maximum each millionaire could have is .5 bitcoin. Bitcoin is so scarce that there isn't even enough bitcoin for each millionaire in the world! What if every person in the world wanted bitcoin? There are 18 million bitcoins and 7.53 billion people in the world as of July 2019. Let's look at how much bitcoin there would be if you allocated bitcoin to each person. So let's divide for this example 18 million/ 7.53 billion which gives us the ridiculously low number of 0.00239043824 bitcoin for each person on the planet. Imagine the potential gains that could possibly be made if you own 1 bitcoin and every person in the world wanted some.

Second reason why I love cryptocurrency is because it makes it easy to send money across the world. If you wanted to send money to Japan from the United States right now through traditional financial systems such as a bank or SWIFT, it would take 3-5 days and it would cost you 10% of the money that you are sending as a fee. Cryptocurrencies allow you to receive and send that same amount of money in a matter of minutes and it costs as little as a couple of pennies to send a million dollars.

Third reason why I love cryptocurrencies and bitcoin is because it can and does serve as a better store of value compared to gold. Now, I know that's a bold claim, so let me back it up with evidence. It's more divisible than gold, easier to carry, easier to track, can be used for day-to-day purchases, and you can literally carry $100 billion dollars by remembering a sequence of numbers and letters. As of 5/2/2019, it is still extremely early, so the potential gains from cryptocurrency is ridiculous. Less than 1% of the world is currently into cryptocurrency, so by every word of the definition, you are an early adapter to the cryptocurrency space. It's like getting into Google stock prices when it was just $10, and now its $1100 as of the time of writing this guide.

Cryptocurrency and bitcoin are already seeing uses across the world. The U.S. Securities and Exchange Commission (SEC) governance system will eventually approve a Bitcoin and Cryptocurrency ETF which will eventually mean that every 401k and/or pension will have bitcoin and cryptocurrencies in it. Some government systems, believe it or not, are talking about using bitcoin and cryptocurrencies as their main financial system and/or as a supplement with their current currency. Cryptocurrencies provide places like Venezuela and Zimbabwe that suffer from hyperinflation a way to safely store their money from a currency that can inflate 10000% in a single year. I wholeheartedly believe that in just about every generational cycle, there is an opportunity provided that is used to decrease the difference in wealth between the rich and the poor. I missed the beginning of the stock market, the industrial age, the dot com area, the silver area, the housing area, so I'll be damned if I miss out on the cryptocurrency era. If it isn't apparent, I believe this is our generational chance to shorten the difference between the rich and the poor and I refuse to miss it.

I want to quickly talk about bitcoin's bull and bear market cycles and what you can expect for the up and incoming bear and bull markets so as not to be caught by surprise. Typically, bitcoin during a bear market corrects by 75-80%, which is more than double of a traditional stock market bear market. The reason for this is because bitcoin and cryptocurrencies are still young and can swing heavily due to the low market cap of 310 billion compared to traditional markets.

We will not try and time the market with bitcoin and cryptocurrency because I believe the best time to invest in an asset that can change the world is now.

Below is a graph of the past bear markets and corrections:

Figure 1: Bitcoin Price Corrections since January 2012 to August 2018
(30% ≤ correction)

Correction Start Date	Correction End Date	# of Days in Correction	Price Recovery End date (i)	Bear Market # of Days in Recovery (i)	Bitcoin High Price	% Change of Previous High	Bitcoin Low Price	% Change of Previous Low	% of Price Decline	$ Difference in Price decline
1/12/12	1/27/12	15	7/12/12	182	$7		$4		-49%	-$4
8/17/12	8/19/12	2	1/21/13	157	$16	55%	$7	46%	-57%	-$9
3/6/13	3/7/13	1	3/18/13	12	$49	67%	$33	78%	-33%	-$16
3/21/13	3/23/13	2	3/25/13	4	$77	36%	$50	34%	-35%	-$27
4/10/13	4/12/13	2	11/6/13	210	$259	70%	$45	-11%	-83%	-$214
11/19/13	11/19/13	1	11/22/13	3	$755	66%	$378	88%	-50%	-$377
11/30/13	1/14/15	410	2/23/17	1181	$1,163	35%	$152	-148%	-87%	-$1,011
3/10/17	3/25/17	15	4/30/17	51	$1,350	14%	$891	83%	-34%	-$459
5/25/17	5/27/17	2	6/6/17	12	$2,760	51%	$1,850	52%	-33%	-$910
6/12/17	7/16/17	34	8/5/17	54	$2,980	7%	$1,830	-1%	-39%	-$1,150
9/2/17	9/15/17	13	10/12/17	40	$4,980	40%	$2,972	38%	-40%	-$2,008
11/8/17	11/12/17	4	11/16/17	8	$7,888	37%	$5,556	47%	-30%	-$2,332
12/17/17	8/14/18	240	As of August 23 2018	249	$19,666	60%	$5,880	6%	-70%	-$13,786
Averages		57		166		43%		28%	-47%	

(i) Price is greater or equal to price on start of correction.
Source: Bitcoincharts.com and DigiCor.io

Let's talk about the past two previous bull markets and the potential return during the third bull market. You couldn't have chosen a better time to invest as of July 2019 because the bear market is over, and the next bull market has begun or is going to begin shortly.

Below is a graph that shows the two previous bull markets of bitcoin. The graph shows the potential growth for the next bull market. As you can see below, the growth for the first bull market was from $2.40 to $1200 and the second bull market was from $245 to $19,000. If you participated in the bull market below, that would be a staggering 50000% return on the first bull market and amazing 7600% on the second bull market. Every bull market that returns drop by a factor of about 6.6, so if we were to divide 7600 by 6.6, we would get a return of 1151% during the next bull market. If we take the yearly low of $3500 and assume that it was the bottom of the bear market, that would result in a price of around $40000 for one bitcoin. Please remember that this is an extremely modest estimate of the potential returns of the next bull market.

Graph of the Previous Two Bull Markets

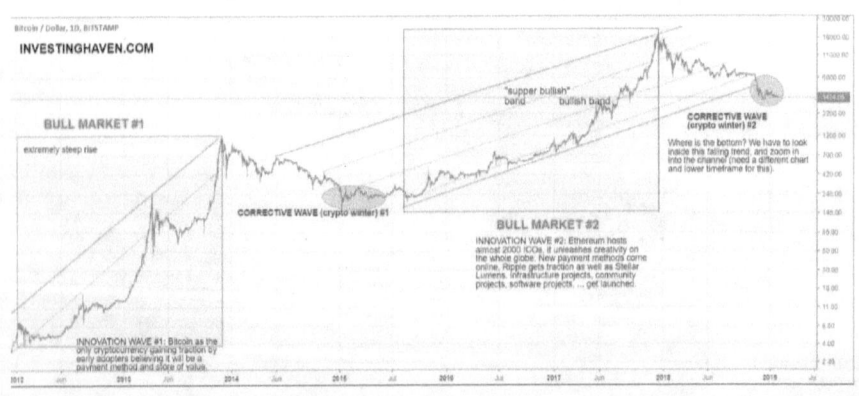

The last point to discuss before getting into the actual allocation of our cryptocurrencies investment portfolio is the long-term potential of something that could replace gold or the world's monetary system. I and many people in cryptocurrency believe at the very least that bitcoin can reach the market cap of gold because it is a better store of value as I proved in a previous section. Gold's market cap is currently eight trillion, and for this example, let's say that bitcoin was to reach this market cap, the price of bitcoin would reach its current market cap of $290 billion, a staggering value of around $250k to $300k per bitcoin. Before we look at the scenario where bitcoin would reach the market cap of the world's reserve currency, I just want to state that I do not actually believe that bitcoin will completely become the world's reserve currency. For this example, let's say that everything is eventually denominated in terms of bitcoin and satoshis. If you are wondering what a satoshi is, it is the lowest possible value that bitcoin can be denominated in. There is 100 million satoshis in a single bitcoin. There is thought that the world's money reserve is as large as 90.8 trillion dollars. If bitcoin was to reach this market cap, that would result in a 3.8-million-dollar bitcoin. I just want to state that this scenario is highly unlikely and should be viewed as a theoretical what-if scenario.

If I haven't convinced you after my long-winded shilling of my love for cryptocurrency, drop your allocation down to 1% and put the other 5.5% into another allocation of our portfolio diversification. I won't allow you to not put at least 1% of your portfolio allocation, you should ALWAYS have some allocation towards cryptocurrency because that 1% could possibly turn into 10% of your total net worth one day. If I have convinced you, I recommend having a buying allocation of 75% allocation of bitcoin, 5% of XRP, 5% Litecoin, 5% of etherum, 5% EOS, and 5% BNB. We have the majority of our cryptocurrency allocation in bitcoin because it is the OG or original of all cryptocurrencies and is the safest out of all options and has built up the most trust.

As you can see, we have diversification on our diversification in cryptocurrencies allocating towards 6 coins in our cryptocurrency portfolio. The main reason why I choose these coins is because they have the most people believing in them, the highest amount of money in them, they have the brightest future, and some of them are already being used by corporations and countries. The reason why we are implementing a hold strategy and not a day trading or swing trading strategy is because it requires a significant number of hours to be good enough to consistently make profit with day trading and/or swing trading. On average, less than 1% of day traders make enough money to replace a 9-5-day job. If you're wondering what day trading and swing trading is, it's the concept of analyzing historical data and trends, indicators, and buy and sell patterns to sell at or buy at a profit. Swing trading has the same principles of day trading, but at a much longer timeframe, for example, a single swing trade can last from weeks to months. You must be extremely good at trading for the returns to outperform holding your digital assets.

Let me briefly discuss why I chose the coins that I did for this portfolio allocation. XRP is an amazing alternative to cross border payment solutions such as SWIFT for sending money across the world. For example, an amazing potential that XRP has is that you can currently send million dollars to any part of the world at a cost of a couple of pennies. Litecoin is a digital equivalent of silver if we use the comparison that bitcoin is digital gold. Ethereum and EOS are smart contract platforms for which every other of the other 2000 cryptocurrencies are built on. In layman's terms, it's the infrastructure for all the other coins in the market. If you're wondering what a smart contract is, a smart contract, also known as a cryptocontract, is a computer program that directly controls the transfer of digital currencies or assets between parties under certain conditions. These contracts are stored on blockchain technology, a decentralized ledger that also underpins bitcoin and other cryptocurrencies. BNB is the equivalent of the New York stock exchange stock of the cryptocurrency space.

We are going to hold onto our cryptocurrencies until the age at which we choose to retire. No different from what we would do with our stock and bond allocation. There are many reasons for holding our cryptocurrencies to the age of retirement; some of the most important ones are avoiding tax implications of selling early, not having stress of constantly monitoring funds, etc. At this point, you're probably thinking I have got you all hyped to buy cryptocurrency but you don't even know how to buy them! Well, you're in luck, because there happens to be a cryptocurrency nerd writing this book that you are currently reading.

I would suggest going to the website, www.coinbase.com; this is one of the most trusted places where you can buy cryptocurrency. Coinbase even has a great guide as to how to buy cryptocurrencies from their exchange.

A link to guide on to how to buy some cryptocurrency is below:

https://www.coinbase.com/buy-bitcoin.

The above guide includes everything that you will need in order to buy your pieces of cryptocurrency. Now that you have some cryptocurrency, you have to store it properly. If you had 100 million dollars in cash, you wouldn't want to store it in your house, because it would likely be stolen and same goes for cryptocurrency. We are going to put it into a safe of sorts, which is something called a ledger wallet. A ledger wallet is an offline digital safe which is safe from hackers and online thieves. If you're interested in the digital ledger and storing your cryptocurrencies offline, you can buy the ledger from Amazon with the link below:

https://www.amazon.com/s?k=ledger+nano+s&crid=1WUH7CVED39OR&sprefix=ledger+%2Caps%2C196&ref=nb_sb_ss_i_2_7

The average cost for the above digital ledger is around $50, but it is worth every penny to securely store your digital ledger offline. The guide below provides you a step-by-step guide for putting cryptocurrency into your Coinbase wallet:

https://www.chainbits.com/cryptocurrencies/how-to-transfer-cryptocurrency/

Even though we are technically holding our cryptocurrencies for the long haul, there is still a strategy associated with holding cryptocurrencies. I understand if you don't want to follow the below strategy, and in that case just hold the cryptocurrency to the age that you choose to retire the same way you would with stocks or bonds. If you're interested in following the holding strategy that I am going to use, please watch every video this guy puts out on bitcoin that I am about to recommend. He talks about taking profits and when you should sell and buy back in. He makes it super simple and he breaks it down to the point where you basically only have to follow a couple of instructions. I love him and highly recommend him above all other people in the cryptocurrency space.

He provides advice on how to dollar cost average into and out the market to guarantee profits, which is important in a volatile market such as cryptocurrency. The link to the guy's YouTube channel is below and once again I can't recommend him highly enough:

https://www.youtube.com/channel/UC0zGwzu0zzCImC1BwPuWyXQ.

I just wanted to state once again that I am obviously not a time traveler and I don't know for certain if cryptocurrencies will live up to my high expectations for them, but if one bitcoin gets past the price of $250,000 thousand, I no longer recommend buying into cryptocurrencies, at that price point. I no longer see an advantageous risk to reward investment structure anymore. At the point that bitcoin reaches $250,000, I recommend putting the money that would be allocated to cryptocurrencies into a different investment or spread out the amount of the rest of the investments stated before. If you wanted an example of how much cryptocurrency that you would potentially own at age 65, the below example provides a decent starting point. Using me as an example, I would have bought anywhere from 100-200k worth of cryptocurrency over my lifetime. This could very well go to zero or has the potential to multiply my money and could be worth 10 to 20 million.

Cryptocurrency is the wildcard of our portfolio and I understand that it is traditionally a much more risky option compared to the other assets, but the risk-to-reward ratio is worth the gamble and I refuse to miss out on the next potential thing to change the world like I did with the internet. If you skipped the previous section, I just want to state that you would be beyond foolish to not put at least 1% of your investment portfolio in cryptocurrency.

INVESTING IN YOURSELF

You're probably thinking, "Why is investing in myself in the investing portfolio section of this guide, shouldn't it be in life tips or a different section?" Well, sorry to tell you that you are sorely wrong; not only is investing in yourself easily the most important part of the portfolio allocation, but it also has the potential to generate you the most passive income, happiness, and satisfaction out of all the rest of the assets combined in the investment portfolio allocation. I know that last statement was a bold statement, because I have stated previously in this chapter that you can easily achieve five million dollars in stocks and bonds and the fact that cryptocurrency has the chance to become the world's currency reserve which would easily multiply your money. My opening statement about the potential returns of investing in yourself is extremely true.

Before we begin talking about investing in yourself, I want to help you visualize why investing in yourself is so important. Let me start by asking you a simple question: Would you a expect a plant to grow bigger if you didn't water it, would you expect an athlete to get better at his craft if he didn't train? Obviously, the answer is no, so why would you expect your dreams, ambitions and goals to come true if you didn't put any effort or money behind it? My dad is a wise man and one of my favorite sayings that he would say is that, "Everyone has a million-dollar idea and a dream to own their business. The ones who have their own business actually started, believed in themselves, and put money behind their dream instead of talking." I want you to force yourself to allocate all 6.5% of this section towards a business idea that you have, bettering yourself with books, attaining skills, knowledge, and trainings.

You may not see any tangible benefits or return on your investment like with the rest of the investments in this chapter, but I promise you that it will be worth every penny. I have met plenty of business owners and the main common denominator as to why they succeeded is that they put money, time, sweat, blood, and tears towards their business ideas. If you're nervous about the potential of opening up your own business, I just want to state that it's okay if at first your business is small and/or not making a lot of money or any at all, because right now, while it is in its infancy stage, we are not expecting it to provide for you. But after you work 10-20 years on a business, invention, or idea that you're truly passionate about, I can almost guarantee that you will be successful with your business and it has the potential to possibly become the largest percentage of your portfolio after years of hard work and dedication.

If you don't have a business idea right now, that's okay; I promise you there will be a time in your life where you will find what you're passionate about if you go about trying to figure that out. You'll only find what you're passionate about if you go out and find what you love to do. If you haven't found your passion yet, I want you to take this 6.5% and do as many things that you think you would like, take as many classes, or trainings as possible to find what you would do for free if money wasn't an issue. Once you find what you're truly passionate about, I want you to think about a way of making money from it while helping as many people with it as humanly possible. For example, for me, I was searching tirelessly for what I'm passionate about, I've literally tried just about anything and everything possible to find out what I love and would do for free. In the meantime, while I was trying to figure out what I truly love, people continually asked me about finances. It then hit me like a brick wall or an epiphany. I thought about the times when

I was the happiest and I realized that it was doing research on finances, helping someone with their finances, or thinking about my own. I thought about how I could help as many people as possible and I came up with the idea about writing this book and to reach out to as many people as humanly possible.

Unfortunately, I don't have any more words of wisdom to help you find what you're passionate about, besides the advice that I gave above. What I can tell you is if there is something that people notice about you or come to you all the time about, that might be a good starting place for you to find your passion.

This section is also for any trainings and skill development classes that you want to take if not stated clearly before. In my case, after I pay off my debt, get a rainy-day fund, and get a 10-20% down payment on my house, I plan to get a culinary degree from a local school (a cheap degree of course), because another passion of mine is cooking vegan food. Eventually, I want to open a vegan restaurant in my area to provide a healthy alternative to the traditionally bad-for-you fast food that most restaurants serve. I also want to get my MBA to learn how to run and manage a business. These skills will take money to get, and instead of going into debt to attain these skills, it is built in and a part of my investment allocation.

Once I get my restaurant up and running, I will be investing money from my portfolio to increase some aspect about the business, whether it's spent on advertisement, paying my employees more, research on new recipes, expanding, etc. If you wouldn't expect a plant to grow without water and sunlight, how do you expect yourself or your business to grow while starving it from resources like money, dedication, and time? How do you expect yourself to grow when you're starving yourself of knowledge and skills you could get by books that you could be reading? I highly recommend buying a book every month with money allocated from this section to learn and grow your passion, to learn a skill that you always wanted to learn, learn about yourself or something you're interested in doing such as learning Spanish. Not only will investing in yourself fuel your soul and improve the quality of your life, it will eventually always fuel your portfolio and provide a huge return on your initial investment once your business or passion starts to blossom.

If you want a couple of ideas of businesses you can try out while you find what you're passionate about, please check out the side hustle section of this guide below. If you're interested in how to start your business, what level of dedication it takes, and or anything else, I highly recommend the book, *The Founder's Dilemmas by Noam Wasserman.*

ANGEL INVESTING/ P2P LENDING
ANGEL INVESTING

Ever seen the TV show, *Shark Tank*? Did you know that the whole premise of that show is angel investing? Of course, some of the parts of that show are dramatized and/or exaggerated, but for the most part, it is an accurate portrayal of how an investor would go about investing in potential startups. You will become a real-life shark in this section of our investment portfolio. This section will require actual time on your behalf and, unfortunately, there isn't an easy strategy to follow for this section, but angel investing has the potential for significant upside if you put the time and the hours in to learn how to properly angel invest.

You might not know it, but there are literally 10,000s if not 100,000s of companies trying to raise capital to try to become the next juggernaut in their particular field. I already know that some of the people reading this guide are probably thinking it is risky. The answer to above statement is yes and no, and I'll discuss below why angel investing is both risky and not risky at the same time. And, of course, once again, that's why we are only putting 6.5% of our allocation towards this investment in case it does not work like we planned it to.

One of my favorite role models, Gary Vaynerchuk, is a multi-millionaire tech advisor that become rich by investing in tech companies when they are startup companies looking for capital to expand and grow. He is one of the best angel investors in the world and has a net worth of over $100 million dollars from angel investing in startup technology companies. He has invested in Google, Snapchat, Venmo, and more during their initial price offering or IPOs. During an IPO, you typically get in when the price of the stock is ridiculously cheap before the product is even released to the public. Gary Vaynerchuk, like I stated before, is one of the most successful angel investors in the world and that being stated his success rate of picking profitable tech companies is around 20%.; one of the most successful angel investors in the world has a success rate of picking profitable startups of around 20%. I already know you're asking how the hell he is turning a profit let alone making millions of dollars annually. Do you know why he can have a 20% success rate of picking successful tech companies to invest in and still make a shit ton of money? The answer is because when he picks a company that is a successful, it's a major success.

For example, let's say he invested 10k each into five companies and three of these companies go bankrupt, so he's out of his 30k on those three companies. One company breaks even, so he keeps his 10k and one company becomes relatively successful and carves out a decent portion of the market they were trying to infiltrate, and as a result the market stock value of that company goes up 10 folds and the stock of that company is now worth 100k. In the above example, on his 50k investment, he made 60k dollars with around a success rate of 20%. This example is an exaggerated case and, it's very unlikely that the three companies would go bankrupt and you would be out of all 30k that you invested. I just wanted to show you a potential case of what type of returns you can potentially gain in the worst case scenario.

How does Gary Vaynerchuk pick startup companies? He looks for both a successful jockey and horse. A jockey in this scenario is the CEO or leader of the startup. The qualities he looks for in a leader, is that he can inspire people, has the motivation, drive, and passion it takes in order to successfully see the company become successful. Some of the questions Gary ask is, does he have the expertise in his particular field to successful carve out a market share? Would this jockey work 24 hours a day if he could to make his company become successful? Does this jockey have qualities of other successful company leaders such as Jack Dorsey, Mark Zuckerberg, or Steve Jobs?

The second thing that Gary Vayerchuk looks for in a potential startup is the horse, which is the actual product. Is the product functional, easy to use, fulfills a need in the market, state-of-the-art technology, has the potential for mass adaption, aspire a sense of awe, already has sales, and would you use the product? Please only ever pick companies that you personally like the product of. Ask yourself if you would buy the product at the price that they are selling it for. Look at their leadership; do you like their leader and would you follow that person? Do they inspire confidence in you when they speak? What do the leaders and companies' long-term goals and dreams look like? What does their finances look like? Is the company in debt or not? What profit are they getting for each item sold? What volume are they experiencing now and expecting in the future? What market are they trying to get into? Do research on the market cap of the market they are trying to in- filtrate and that will tell you the potential top of that particular market. For example, if your company wants to carve a market share out of the used meat market, the potential growth of that company might be limited.

Another rule that Gary Vayerchuk and other angel investors implement is that they never put more than 10% of their money allocated for angel investing into one company. You already know we must have diversification on our portfolios! What I recommend is to split the allocation for angel investing portion between 10 companies that you actually believe in and stick with them until they mature into the companies that the company has envisioned for them. This way, you're not putting all of your eggs in one basket, so if some of these companies go bankrupt or don't do well, you can still make money.

Below is a chart of some of the most successful Technology IPOs and Gary Vayerchuk has invested in most of them:

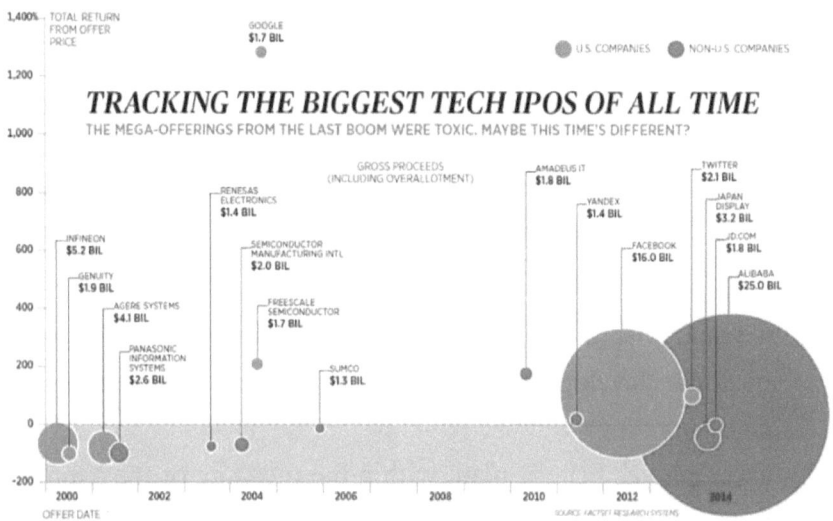

Where do you go in order to start angel investing? Well, thankfully, we live in the internet age and we don't have to necessarily meet the leader of the company in person, which I would do if applicable and possible to get a better sense of the jockey. I recommend using the websites AngelList or SeedInvest to find startups looking for investment funds. These websites are safe and have millions of dollars invested through them daily. These websites will allow you to start with a lower amount of capital, which will allow you to angel invest monthly instead of saving up a lump sum to start angel investing. These websites are great because they give you a wide array of startups looking for your investments, they are easy to use, and they provide a basis for you to start doing research on these companies and start your own angel investing empire like Gary Vayerchuk!

Here are links to both AngeList and SeedInvest: https://angel.co/ and https://www.seedinvest.com/

The only thing that might stop you from angel investing is that typically to take part in IPOs, you have to be an accredited investor. In the United States, to be considered an accredited investor, one must have a net worth of at least $1,000,000, excluding the value of one's primary residence, or have income at least $200,000 each year for the last two years (or $300,000 combined income if married) and have the expectation to make the same amount this year. The term "accredited investor" is defined in Rule 501 of Regulation D of the U.S. Securities and Exchange Commission (SEC) as:

1. a bank, insurance company, registered investment company, business development company, or small business investment company;
2. an employee benefit plan, within the meaning of the Employee Retirement Income Security Act, if a bank, insurance company, or registered investment adviser makes the investment decisions, or if the plan has total assets in excess of $5 million;
3. a charitable organization, corporation, or partnership with assets exceeding $5 million;
4. a director, executive officer, or general partner of the company selling the securities;
5. a business in which all the equity owners are accredited investors;
6. a natural person who has individual net worth, or joint net worth with the person's spouse, that exceeds $1 million at the time of the purchase, or has assets under management of $1 million or above, excluding the value of the individual's primary residence;
7. a natural person with income exceeding $200,000 in each of the two most recent years or joint income with a spouse exceeding

$300,000 for those years and a reasonable expectation of the same income level in the current year; or
8. a trust with assets in excess of $5 million, not formed to acquire the securities offered, whose purchases a sophisticated person makes."

Don't worry, there is no paperwork that you will have to submit to be considered an accredited investor. The process of verifying that you are an accredited investor depends entirely on the company that you are trying to become part of. Individuals who feel they qualify can visit a fund and ask for information about potential investments. At this time, the issuer of securities will give a questionnaire to determine whether a person qualifies as an "accredited investor." The questionnaire will also likely require the attachment of financial statements and information of other accounts in order to verify the ownership of assets listed on a balance sheet like the one above. Companies will also likely evaluate a credit report in order to assess any debts held by a person seeking accredited status. Individuals who base their qualifications on annual income will likely need to submit tax returns, W-2 forms, and other documents that indicate wages. Individuals may also consider letters from reviews by CPAs, tax attorneys, investment brokers, or advisors.

Following this guide, you will quickly become an accredited investor and be able to start angel investing! The reason why you need to be an accredited investor is because angel investing is seen as risky and the United States Government as well as other government systems want the person investing to be good with finances and money to make rational decisions when it comes to angel investing.

I want to briefly talk about investing in a friend or acquaintance's idea or startup company. I want to make it crystal clear that just because you are friends, or you know this person does not mean that you will treat them or their business any different from any other startup or leader of that company. You will ask the same questions as you would any

CEO of a startup. If you don't feel good about any of the replies to the questions that you asked, don't invest in them.

P2P LENDING

If becoming an angel investor scares you or you don't have the time to do research on potential companies and CEOs, there is a lower maintenance alternative that still has potential for consistent returns. The alternative to angel investing that we will discuss is called P2P lending or peer to peer lending. The concept of peer to peer lending, in layman's term, translates to the fact that you essentially become a bank for people looking for a loan for various reasons. You can average annually an 8% return on your initial investment with little to medium risk using P2P lending.

How peer to peer lending works in some of the P2P lending websites below is that it takes the amount of money that you allocate for P2P lending and divides that amount into smaller quantities to manage your potential risk of any single default of a loan significantly impacting your potential return on your investment and allocates these small quantities at different risk levels. This is to provide diversification within your loans and to provide you with the highest possible interest rate while keeping your risk lower.

It does this by using its algorithms to balance between the risk of the loan and the interest rate of that loan; an example would be that the higher the risk of a loan, the higher interest rate you can expect on that loan.

Links to P2P lending websites that are popular and that are trustworthy are below:

https://www.upstart.com/ and https://www.fundingcircle.com/.

One thing that you will have to consider when it comes to P2P lending is that people can default on your loan, which means they don't pay back your money. Thankfully, this is rare because it damages their credit, and they get blackballed from multiple P2P lending sites, and they are typically prevented from ever using that site again. The average de- fault rate is around 1 out of 100 loans or 1%. Your interest rate that you're receiving on the rest of the loans that did not default will highly outweigh the one or two loan defaults that you would experience during investing. For example, let's say you put 10k on a lending P2P site to start investing, the lending website would allocate the 10k into hundred $100 dollars loans at an average of a 7-8% annual return on your money. If one of these one hundred dollar loans defaults, you're out of a 100% of that loan which translates to 100 dollars lost, but you got an 8% average annual return on the rest of the 99, so you made on average, $800.

Let me ask you the question, are you really that upset that the one loan defaulted when you made eight times the loss that you experienced?

QUICK SUMMARY FOR INVESTMENT SECTION

To conclude the previous chapter about investing, I just want to restate why I chose each of the above investments and the allocations that I did. I choose stocks and bonds because it has a great return of around 10% with low risk and plenty of historical data to provide confidence that it is going to be around for a long time. Cash for any one-in-a-lifetime investing opportunity that might pop up. Gold and silver as a hedge against the traditional financial systems and a potential for great returns during an economic recession or economic downtime. Cryptocurrencies because they have the potential upside to easily 10x to 100x your initial investment. Investing in yourself/business/passion because it can and will eventually provide you an opportunity to make money doing something you love. Angel Investing/ P2P Lending for a high potential for amazing returns or P2P lending for a safe alternative that averages around 8% at fairly low risk.

By the age of 65, I can expect around five million dollars in stocks and bonds, 200k in cash reserves, around 200k in physical gold and silver, 200k allocated to cryptocurrency, 200k that I have invested in myself to learn any skills or grow a business to become successful, and 200k allocated towards angel investing or 200k in P2P lending. None of the above statements consider appreciation of assets besides stocks and bonds. Each of these 200k allocated investment sections can grow as much as 5-10 times what you allocated towards them.

There are dozens of other opportunities of investing, but I believe that I have provided the best mix of investments to maximize returns, keep risk low, and have the potential to create life-changing wealth over time. This is all without the biggest passive income generator which I will talk about in a later step, real estate.

Below is a chart that shows my allocation towards these investments and my expected return at age 40, 50, and 65.

Age 65 Allocation and Expected Returns

Type of Investment	% of investment allocation	Allocated Investment Total	Expected Value at age 65
Stocks and Bonds	62.5%	1 million dollars	5 million dollars
Cash	6.5%	200k	500k
CryptoCurrency	6.5%	200k	500k
Investing in Yourself	6.5%	200k	1 million dollars
Gold/Silver	6.5%	200k	500k
P2P Lending	6.5%	200k	300k
Angel Investing	6.5%	200k	500k

The above graph shows a modest model of what I can expect at the traditional retirement age of 65. I will have five million dollars in stocks and bonds, 500k in cash or investments opportunities derived from that cash, a million dollars generated from investing in myself, passion, or business ideas that I might have, and 500k in gold and silver, due to the appreciation of the value of both gold and silver. If I chose to go with P2P lending instead of angel investing, I would expect 300k at the age of 65. If I choose to go with angel investing instead of P2P lending, I would expect the investment to grow to the size of 500k. This is all a very conservative estimate of what I would expect at the age of 65. If the above scenario happens, which I am almost assuredly sure that it will, I will have over 8 million dollars' worth of investments by the age of 65.

STEP ONE OF REAL ESTATE TRAIN
ACQUIRE A 3-BEDROOM 2-BATH HOUSE

This section comes after paying off our debt and saving for our emergency fund. This is the next big step in preparing ourselves for financial independence and freedom. This will start our process of our "Real Estate Train" and our passive income journey. I know I've been hyping up the Real Estate Train for the last twenty pages, but I promise you it was worth the wait. First step to the Real Estate Train is finding a 3-bedroom 2-bath house in the area that you want to live in and saving close to 20% of its cost for a down payment as possible. The reason why we are shooting for 20% is because we will pay this house off very quickly and 20% down payment equates to less time that we are making payments to pay off this house and putting a large down payment gives us the power to negotiate a much better mortgage interest rate.

I recommend living at least 30 minutes out of any major city in order to keep the price of your house down to something reasonable. The reason why we are looking particularly for a 3-bedroom 2-bath house is because we will rent this place out for passive income when we eventually move into a larger home to accommodate for a wife and kids. You can get a higher premium for rent if the house has 3 bedrooms and 2 baths; this is the sweet spot for beginner rental properties because it holds its resale value better than non-3-bedroom 2-bath places and anything beyond a 3-bedroom and 2 baths would take too long to pay off and accumulate 20% for a down payment.

Using myself as an example, I want to live in Lawrenceville, which is 40 minutes outside the city of Atlanta. I choose Lawrenceville even though it is 40 minutes out from the city of Atlanta because I want to avoid paying crazy prices for living within the city perimeter. An example of what the typical cost, at least, in Georgia would be for a 3-bedroom 2-bath is around 130,000 thousand dollars. If I was to save 20%, that would be 26k that I will save before I get a mortgage on that home. I would use websites and apps such as Zillow, Truila, and home finder.

Here are the links to these websites: https://www.zillow.com/ and https://www.trulia.com/ and https://homefinder.com/.

These apps and websites show you houses for sale in your desired living location and has indicators if the price it is listed for is a good deal. You should also consider duplexes when searching for a starter home or rental property. A duplex is a house that is split into two units so that two people can live there. It essentially allows you to have two renters at once. If you were to find a duplex for $130,000, you could charge each tenant
$800 each increasing your monthly rent by more than 20%! I personally don't like duplexes because they make it extremely hard to do a rent-to-own lease, which I will talk about later in this chapter.

For our real estate train, we are going to only buy pretty houses instead of ugly houses. A pretty house is a house that requires little to no work, whereas an ugly house comes with a great deal of issues that require, at least, 20,000 dollars' worth of work before it becomes hospitable to a potential renter.

I could go into extreme detail about what to look for in a house, but I would rather leave it up to someone who writes more elegantly than me.

Here is the link to buying homes: https://lifehacker.com/the-start-to-finish-guide-to-buying-a-home-1663317601.

Make sure to pay for a home inspector to inspect any home that you are thinking about buying to make sure there isn't any additional work that wasn't explained to you or that you weren't expecting. If you are still having trouble finding a place to fit in your budget, please strongly consider getting a real estate agent; they are worth the money it costs to find you the house that you are looking for. If there are additional repairs or damages that needs to be done, subtract the additional repair cost from the price you were willing to pay and ask the owner for a discount on top of the repair cost. If they refuse to give you this discount, walk away from the deal and continue your search.

Before you go and get a mortgage for your starter home, it is imperative to make sure that you have excellent credit. That requirement should not be an issue because we have been building our credit for the last 3-5 years while paying off debt, saving for a rainy-day fund, and saving for a 20% down payment. This goes without saying, but make sure that you have paid off all of your debts prior to getting a mortgage for a home. This is ensuring that your debt-to-income ratio remains low, which will help in negotiating a lower interest rate on your mortgage. Having excellent credit, not being in debt, and having a quality job that has a salary of at least 50k will guarantee that that you get a mortgage.

I understand the following statement sounds crazy, but 40% of Americans don't even qualify to get a bank mortgage. You will not only qualify for a mortgage, banks will literally be fighting to give you a mortgage. After you acquire the down payment needed for your start home, it's officially time to get a mortgage for the remaining 80% in order to purchase the house. We are going to use the previous statements of having excellent credit, no debt, a good job, and a large down payment to our advantage to get a great interest rate. During the process of getting a mortgage, a couple of things to negotiate are to make sure that they can't come after you after the house is foreclosed on. Negotiate the closing close and try to get rid of any additional bullshit fees that they try and tack on.

Always get a fix-rate loan so interest rates don't increase on you. Ask them what the Annual Percentage Rate and Interest Rate is and if they can lower it. Ask for the cost of each of the following items and reduce as many of these as possible: appraisal, credit report, lender title policy, pest inspection reports, escrow, recording fees, and taxes. Ask if they offer loan rate locks. When you are ready to get a mortgage, print out the list of questions provided in the link below and ask ALL of them, and I guarantee if you ask every question on the list, there's no way in hell that you won't get the best interest rate and get the loan on the best terms possible. Your goal during your hearing for getting a mortgage is to get your interest rate to as close to 3% as possible; 3.5% is a reasonable interest rate to shoot for as of July 2019.

Fair interest rates for people like us vary vastly with the current state of your country's economy. A link to check what interest rates you can expect in your country is below, it has monthly updates to help the below information stay relevant:

https://www.bankrate.com/mortgage.aspx.

Below is a link for tips and things to ask for negotiating for during mortgage talks:

https://www.theglobeandmail.com/real-estate/mortgages-and-rates/the-ultimate-mortgage-checklist-63-steps-to-navigating-the-best-deal/article14868520/.

We are only going to get 10-year mortgages because it will give us the lowest possible mortgage interest rate, and we want to pay the house off as soon as possible, the lower the mortgage interest rates, the better. The reason why we don't get mortgages below ten years is because we don't get a reduction on interest rates below that and staying at the ten-year mortgage gives you some flexibility with a lower mortgage payment in case something comes up, so you don't have to struggle to pay the payments. I have found that 10 years is the sweet spot for the number of years because it incentives us to pay off the mortgage quickly, gives us the best possible interest rate, and gives us flexibility with payments if a financial crisis comes up. Our goal will be to pay the lowest amount of interest on our newly acquired ten-year mortgage, and in order to accomplish this goal that we have set for ourselves, we will be making double monthly mortgage every month minus the monthly cost for house insurance.

There are a couple of reasons that we are doing this: one is to pay off the house as quickly as possible and to reduce the amount of money we are paying in interest, and two, this allows us to build up real estate properties debt-free to create a passive income stream!

Using the house I want to buy as an example, my monthly payments would be around $950, so if we double that, it would be $1900 minus $50 dollars for house insurance, which means I will send the bank $1850 in monthly payments until the mortgage is paid off. The time it will take to pay off your mortgage, in this example, will be less than half of ten years due to the fact that we are cutting the potential interest acquired on the loan in half which will save us a couple months of additional payments!

Below is an example of the type of money that you can save in interest by making double payments on a ten year mortgage:

Example of Interest Saved with Double Payments

Mortgage repayment shortened by 5 years and 1 month

Mortgage payoff inputs:		Total savings $10,091
Years remaining:	10 years	
Original mortgage term:	10 years	
Original mortgage amount:	$104,000	
Additional principal payment:	$900	
Annual interest rate:	3.5%	
Report amortization:	Annually / Monthly	

Mortgage payoff result summary:	
Current payment: $1,028.41	Scheduled payments: $123,410
Accelerated payment: $1,928	Accelerated payments: $113,319

If you're interested in calculating the amount of interest you would save by making double payment, the link I used in my example is below.

Link to early loan payment calculator: https://www.bankrate.com/calculators/mortgages/mortgage-loan-payoff-calculator.aspx

In this example, you saved 10k by making double payments! You just started the real estate train and have acquired your first piece of what will be the building block of a system that will generate a life-changing stream of passive income. I just want to state again that any real estate, including rental properties, is to be considered when you are calculating your net worth, but was added to the portfolio investment allocation strategy in the previous chapter, because it deserves its own investing allocation and it makes up an entirely different portion of our budget and our monthly expenses and income allocation.

The reason why it will take you a couple months sooner than what you would expect to pay off your mortgage is because the bank builds the ten-year mortgage with the expected interest acquired over ten years. If you can't afford to make double payments on this mortgage, put down as much as you possibly can every month. Even if you were to allocate an extra $100 every month towards your mortgage, you would still pay the mortgage off faster than the bank's allotted ten-year period and you would have saved yourself some money in interest.

If you don't have a wife or kids or live-in girlfriend, I highly suggest getting a roommate to live with you, because it's essentially free money if you can stand to live with someone. This will give you additional money to help pay off your mortgage quicker or it will make it so that you can make double payments in the first place. If you plan to get a roommate, I highly suggest getting a month-to-month lease, so you can kick them out anytime you feel ready. Trust me, it will be nice to have the flexibility to kick out your roommate. For example, if you get married, have kids, or get a girlfriend that wants to live with you or you get tired of living with someone, you'll want the flexibility to kick them out at the end of the month.

If you're planning to get a roommate, please read and reference this guide about how to structure and manage a month to month lease.
https://www.rocketlawyer.com/article/how-a-month-to-month-rental-agreement-works-cb.rl.

Once you pay off your starter home, congrats, you no longer have any reason to ever be in debt again if you choose not to! The allocated double payments that you were making towards your mortgage payment will now be put monthly in a high-yield saving or money market account to start saving for your first rental property. You are now well on your way towards financial freedom and independence.

STEP TWO OF REAL ESTATE TRAIN

(Step Two: Acquire two rental property 10-year mortgages and pay them off in three years and two years)

A couple of tips before we delve into buying a rental property. I suggest only buying houses in towns or neighborhoods you are familiar with that also have good public schools. This will prevent you from buying a house in the wrong neighborhood with poor resale value or rentability. Make sure the neighborhood you are considering buying a rental property in has houses that look presentable and well-kept. A golden question to ask yourself when looking to buy a rental property is if you would live in this neighborhood or not. This will minimize the risk that the rental property you are planning to buy or buying will keep its resale value and be rentable for many years to come into the future. If you buy a house in a neighborhood, you're not familiar with and bad public schools around, you very well could lose money on your rental property from a lack of good tenants and depreciation.

A couple core concepts and things that you must consider when you start looking for a rental property is that, like I stated before, it must contain at least 3 bedrooms and 2 baths. Look for homes that are accessible by train and bus and that have shopping and movie theaters nearby. You should look for rental properties where houses in that area average a yield at least 1% return on the house value every month in rent. For example, if a house is worth $130,000, you should aim to get around $1300 in rent monthly. Please do research on rental properties in this neighborhood, and if they are not averaging close to 1% of the house value in rent monthly, don't buy this rental property and look for one that is averaging as close to 1% as humanely possible. Another thing to consider is to make sure that the neighborhood you're expecting to buy a house in doesn't have a high home owner association fees. Please do research on what a reasonable home owner association fee is for you and your area.

For example, in the area that I am currently looking to buy a house, I would refuse to pay more than 500 dollars a year in home owner association fees on a 130 thousand dollars house. If I lived in New York city, I would be ecstatic to only have to pay 500 dollars a year in Home Owner Association Fees, so the location you get a house in can vastly vary how much you should expect to pay in home owner association fees.

If you are interested in more qualities that you should look for in a rental property, I will link a website below that goes in depth about this topic:

Link to buying your first rental property: https://fitsmallbusiness.com/buying-your-first-rental-property-tips/.

Before we talk more about getting two rental properties, let's talk about the concept of a real estate train and why it will take four and a half years to acquire the first rental property and three and a half years to acquire the second rental property.

Imagine it's like a train and that with every real estate property that you acquire, you are gaining momentum and using that momentum to propel yourself forward at an accelerated rate. Let's expand on this idea by thinking of a train that is trying to reach maximum speed. Trains take some time to get up to full power, but once they get going, they are almost impossible to stop. Let's take that concept and apply it to real estate. Just like with the train, it is going to take a while to get up to full speed or acquire the first couple of properties, but after that, each rental property that we will acquire and pay off will build momentum and decrease the time that it will take to acquire the next rental property. Using myself as an example, I have estimated that it would take around four years to acquire my first rental property home.

Using the links I provided before in this chapter, buy your first rental property and calculate how long it will take you to save up for another rental property. During your calculation this time instead of putting an interest rate of around 3.5%, put a 0% interest rate because we will be buying houses with cash from now on to stay debt-free. While saving up money to buy these houses, put the cash you are saving in a high-yield money market or savings accounts to help ward off the threat of inflation. Our second rental property using the calculator I have provided before will take us around three years to pay off. The reason for this, is because each time we acquire a new rental property, any income that we receive from the rental property through means of rent will go towards saving for the next rental property.

For example, let's say we currently are saving $1800 from our previous mortgage payment plus receiving $800 for rent after accounting for potential costs associated with renting and owning a house which I will talk about in great detail later, from our first rental property, that equates to $2600 monthly going towards buying a second rental property. After we acquire a second rental property and rent it out, we are now saving
$3200 monthly towards rental properties, then with the acquisition of a third rental property $4000 will be allocated monthly to save for another rental property, and so on and so on.

For the above reason, I call it the real estate train, because each new rental property we acquire will decrease the time it will take to buy another rental property cash. You will eventually get to the point where you will be able to buy a new rental property in less than a year or have the equivalent of having $130,000 worth of passive income every year from rental properties alone! Examples of the calculations I used to figure out how long it will take me to buy my first and second rental properties are below:

Calculation for time period for acquisition of first rental property

Mortgage repayment shortened by 6 years and 1 month

Mortgage payoff inputs:

- Years remaining: 10 years
- Original mortgage term: 10 years
- Original mortgage amount: $130,000
- Additional principal payment: $1,700
- Annual interest rate: 0%
- Report amortization: ● Annually ○ Monthly

Total savings $0

Mortgage payoff result summary:
Current payment: $1,083.33
Accelerated payment: $2,783
Scheduled payments: $130,000
Accelerated payments: $130,000

Calculation for time period for acquisition for second rental property

Mortgage repayment shortened by 6 years and 11 months

Mortgage payoff inputs:

- Years remaining: 10 years
- Original mortgage term: 10 years
- Original mortgage amount: $130,000
- Additional principal payment: $2,500
- Annual interest rate: 0%
- Report amortization: ● Annually ○ Monthly

Total savings $0

Mortgage payoff result summary:
Current payment: $1,083.33
Accelerated payment: $3,583
Scheduled payments: $130,000
Accelerated payments: $130,000

Now that you understand how the real estate train works, let's talk about how to properly acquire your two rental properties, which will be the foundation for all the passive income that you will need to make you financially independent and begin your journey to financial freedom. I suggest that you get a rental property for the same price that you bought your starter home for, with the same qualities as your starter home to keep things simple, and for the fact that you now have some expertise in buying this particular type of house. I want to quickly restate that, being financially independent does not mean that you can be reckless with your money, it simply means that you have more passive income coming in than monthly expenses. This means that you can quit your job and still be able to pay all the monthly bills on time, but not live a life of excessive luxuries.

Some of you are probably questioning why we are buying rental properties with cash, when we can put a renter in the house while we have a mortgage for and acquire, essentially, extra cash. The above statement is a 100% percent true statement and mathematically a better option compared to buying rental properties with cash. There are two reasons why I wouldn't suggest it for the common man. Reason one is that you are assuming some risk, taking on a mortgage with a bank that may or may not be reliant on how steady your tenants are. The second reason is that you will always be in debt to the bank if you are currently taking on a new mortgage every time you want to acquire a new rental property mortgage. These two reasons are why I believe that 95% of people should stick to buying rental properties with cash. If you don't mind the two points that I stated before and hate to see any potential money left like me, the next paragraph is for you.

In the name of clarity, I do plan to get a mortgage on the property that I am renting out and currently paying off, because I hate to see potential money left on the table. I want to make it 100% clear that if you follow the strategy of getting mortgages on a rental property you are currently paying off, to never ever have more than one mortgage open at one time, this is to mitigate the possibility of being overleveraged.

If you choose to open a mortgage on a rental property, we are going to use the exact steps that we used to get a mortgage for our starter home. A summary of that was putting 20% as a down payments, asking all 64 essential questions provided, and getting the cheapest interest rate possible. When buying still think about location, potential rent, and etc. . The only difference that should be between a rental property and a starter home is that there is a renter in the rental property and that you are mortgaging to get an additional extra mortgage payment to pay off the house sooner. This equates to an additional $800 per month that we wouldn't have received otherwise.

Once you acquire a rental property, get your first tenants, and start getting rent from them, it's tempting to pocket all the rent money that you are getting, which in my particular example would be $1300. This however would be failing to do the golden rule of this book, which is if you fail to plan, you plan to fail. What I mean by this is that if you were to pocket all the $1300 of the rent that you are receiving, you are failing to plan for paying for home owner insurance, property taxes, landscaping cost, unforeseen repairs, management fees, and potential damage done by tenants. In order to plan for this, we are going to save as close to 40% as possible of all incoming rent to cover the cost that we just discussed. For example, if you are getting $1300 in rent on a $130,000- home, you would put around $500 in a money market account for any of the above cost that we discussed previously.

You should also make it mandatory that all tenants have renter's insurance to help cover your ass in case of theft and damages to their property in your rental home. Let's briefly discuss a point of contention that A lot of you reading probably have. The point that I don't want to be a landlord, or I don't know how to be a landlord or how to find good tenants. I understand that the task of being a landlord or finding good tenants can be a daunting task, but don't worry I'll provide some links or an alternative solution to solve your concerns.

Below is the link to a guide that teaches you to be an effective landlord and how to find good tenants.

Link to being a good landlord: https://www.landlordology.com/first-time-landlord-tips/

Guide to getting good tenants: https://www.thebalancesmb.com/the-right-tenant-for-your-rental-2124984

If you plan to be a landlord and not use a rental property management company, let me give you a couple of tips that are not in the guide that I have linked above. If you like the tenants and they respect your property and always pay on time, I would advise to try and not raise rent on them because having a good tenant is worth losing a one hundred or two hundred dollars in potential rent that can be gained by raising rent cost every month. I do not plan to become a landlord because, I do not have the time currently to become an landlord, because I am trying to turn my passion for finance into something that is generating me income. The approach I will take instead is to get a management company that manages putting tenants in your house, collection of rent, upkeeping the property, and managing any repairs that might be needed with your property. Nothing in life is free and, typically, management companies charge 10% of the monthly rent that you would receive as well as the first month's entire rent when they place a new tenant in the home. This new fee which is about one month's worth of rent, is only applied once every couple of years with the signing of a new lease with a new tenant.

If you plan to use a rental property management company, try to save 45% instead of 40% from monthly rent to accommodate for the cost associated with the rental property. I will link a guide to using a rental property management company and typically how much they cost below.

Link to rental property management: https://learn.roofstock.com/blog/how-much-do-property-managers-charge.

I will not be doing a strictly normal renting though; I plan to turn every single one of my rental properties into rent to home rental properties. There are a couple of reasons for this: number one, you are helping people potentially own or live in a house that they typically couldn't and wouldn't be able to afford. The number two reason for rent-to-own rental properties is that they can be more profitable compared to traditional rental properties. Rent-to-own properties gives the option to the renter to buy the rental property once all the agreed upon criteria is meet.

Even though the differences between a rent-to-own and a traditional rental property may be small, the ramifications of the differences between the two are gigantic.

For starters, there is a mandatory one-time option to buy-fee that is typically 3-5% of the house's worth. That's essentially another 5-10k in your pocket, just because you choose to do rent-to-own instead of a traditional rental property. Typically, rent-to-home properties have a mandatory period that the renter must rent for before they have the option to buy. This can be negotiable, but I recommend anywhere from three to five years before the option to buy the house kicks in. Another great feature about rent-to-own properties is that any damages are presumably taken care of by your renter. This is also negotiable, but I would insist that this be part of your arrangement.

Some additional benefits are that you can typically offer higher sales prices even in a soft market. You can charge a higher rent because part of a rent-to-own contract is that a part of the rent goes towards reducing the price of the house when the renter is ready to buy the house. The percentage that goes towards this is also negotiable as well. I recommend that 10% of rent that you receive goes towards reducing the cost of the house.

One of the negatives of the rent-to-own is that you must lock in a price that must be kept if the renter meets the requirement to buy the house. My favorite part of rent-to-own, and a major boon for our strategy of owning properties debt-free, is that once they are able to buy the house, they can get financing to buy the house from you! Whatever their bank quoted interest rate for a mortgage is for your renter, beat it by .5% to make sure that they finance through you. A renter financing through you is like P2P lending on steroids. If the renter chooses to finance through you, you would be getting a compounding 4-5% interest yearly on a house that would typically be going towards a bank. This agreement of you financing them gives you all the same protections that a bank would have.

Some of these protections include: if they fail to make payments, you can legally kick them out and get another tenant. All the monthly payments, the buy-fee, and rent, interest, and the house are yours to keep. The only potential downside of this is that you would have to legally evict your tenant and potentially might have to take them to court. The potential upside highly outweighs the fringe scenario where you must take a tenant to court. If the renter completely pays off the house, use the money gained through this to buy another house and repeat the above process. I just want to state that the chances of a renter renting from you for the allocated time period, and paying off the house completely is extremely low, and if they break the contract at any point, you get to keep the house and all the other benefits discussed above.

If you're interested in rent-to-own and want more information, I have provided a link below:

https://www.trulia.com/guides/how-does-rent-to-own-work/.

I would recommend that you hire a real estate lawyer to draft a rent-to-own contract for each new tenant. This is to ensure you don't miss anything, and that the contract includes everything that you want.

I want to briefly talk about the differences between Airbnb and renting, because I already know some people are planning to turn their rental properties into Airbnbs. If you're not familiar with Airbnb, it's a company that essentially allows you to turn your rental properties into a hotel or hostel. Through the Airbnb website, you advertise your house to hundreds of thousands of people that can choose if they want to stay at your place for as little as a day, week, or months. Even though there might be minor differences between the two, these minor differences have serious implications.

If you were to take the Airbnb route, you are now more in the hospitality and customer service business than the renting business; this is due to the fact that your Airbnb business thrives on the satisfaction of your customers. You must maintain a high rating on Airbnb or you will not do well on the platform. This difference turns the traditionally passive source of income of renting into a part time job. Don't believe me? I'll briefly describe some of the things that are required to be successful in the Airbnb business.

You must constantly respond to inquiries asking about booking a stay at your rental property. You must furnish the rental property with amenities for living and maintain them. You must maintain check-ins and check-outs constantly for each new guest. You must clean your rental property after every guest stay, which can take a significant amount of time if you don't hire a cleaner. You must constantly go on supply runs to stock your rental properties with amenities such as toilet paper, soap, toothpaste, etc. You must be able to be flexible for emergencies such as lockouts or plumbing incidents. You constantly must think about catering to your audiences and comparing your rates with other Airbnbs and other local hotels to stay competitive. Even though maintaining an Airbnb sounds is a lot of work, there is a huge monetary upside when it comes to them compared to rental properties.

If you can successfully set up an Airbnb business, you can essentially double what you would be getting for rent. Instead of only getting $1300 for rent monthly, for a $130,000 property, you could easily get $2600 a month from the same property using Airbnb. You will have to make the decision if turning your passive income stream into a side hustle is worth doubling the effective rent that you are receiving.

If you choose to turn your rental properties into Airbnb properties, I have included below a couple of tips that my friend, who is a successful Airbnb host, implements:

Make sure that any listing on the Airbnb platform has a quality title, description, host profile, and professionally shot photographs. You only ever get one first impression when it comes to Airbnbs; make sure you start strong to build up positive reviews. You never want to make an unannounced visit on your customers; absolutely nobody likes their privacy to be invaded. Make sure to avoid squatters and other risky guests, because damages and potential lawsuits are not worth the potential money that you could get off these types of customers. Make sure that you protect your property and identity so as not to make yourself a target. You need to have dynamic pricing based on events, days of the week, and competitors pricing. Always put an extra bed in your Airbnb than you would think necessary, because it allows you to book more people at your property at any given time.

Always have white linens where applicable. Customers love them because it a sense of confirmation that your Airbnb is completely clean. You should have different amenities such as coffee makers, candles, and hair dryers to instill a feeling of home in your customers. You should provide a small gift for every guest; you'll be surprised how many good reviews you receive for just giving them a small gift.

Even though I personally don't plan to turn my rental properties into Airbnbs, that doesn't mean that I don't think Airbnbs aren't a good idea. I am just infatuated with the idea of passive income, and Airbnbing would turn my rental properties into a side hustle. I do plan to implement something similar for my vacation home though. If you also plan to eventually get a vacation home, I only suggest getting a vacation home once you have reached financial freedom or independence. Obviously, I will only ever get this vacation home once I have reached financial independence and freedom. Even though a vacation home is an unnecessary luxury, I still plan to turn it into a source of passive income. How I plan to do this is by implementing a special type of renting/AirbNbing, which is the equivalent of doing a long term AirbNb, while I am not at the vacation home. This will essentially allow me to turn my vacation home into another rental property, while giving me the flexibility of using it as a vacation home whenever I want.

The service that I plan to implement to do this is HomeAway. One of the only negatives of this service is that there is a $349-subscription fee, but I assure you that it is well worth the price tag. HomeAway allows you to list your properties on three websites with one listing and the application is centered around longer stays lasting anywhere from a month to a year. Implementing the system of longer visits of my vacation home allows me to get a rental property manager. The rental property manager will handle the business of being a landlord, which turns my vacation home into another source of passive income.

If you want more information when it comes to turning your rental properties into Airbnbs, please see the below link:

https://www.passiveairbnb.com/airbnb-hosting-guide/

If you want more information when it comes to turning your vacation house into a rental property, please use the below guide:

https://www.washingtonian.com/2016/02/18/you-can-find-renters-to-pay-off-your-vacation-house-airbnb-vrbo-homeaway/

Congrats you have reached financial independence with the acquisition of your starter home and your two rental properties. You should have no debt and have at least $1600 dollars in passive income coming in every month. If you stick to the budget that we created way earlier in a previous chapter, this should outweigh your monthly expenses, so you technically don't have to work a job anymore. Not only are you financially independent, but you also have many more things to feel accomplished and proud about. Let me list the accomplishments that you have achieved thus far on your 12-15 year journey of following the steps of this book. You have acquired a great job that pays you what you are worth, you have excellent credit, you don't have any car payments, you have at least 100k in assets if not more in your investment portfolio, you are the owner of three paid off houses, two of which are generating passive income for you, you have 10-20k in your savings/ money market account as a rainy-day fund, and you have learned how to manage and budget money effectively. You also have absolutely zero debt and have more passive income coming in than monthly expenses. I just want to state, that last accomplishment is something of that 90% of Americans never reach. You no longer must work a day job any longer and can follow your dreams and not worry about how your bills will get paid every month. You have a net worth of half a million dollars and are on your way towards becoming an accredited investor.

Like I have stated before, I still recommend you work even though you technically don't have to. On the topic of continuing working, You can take one of the below avenues: you can continue working for someone else and rise through the corporate ladder some more, you can start your own business about what you're passionate about, or you can take some time off to do some of the things that you always wanted to do.

After acquiring financial independence, it is a time to make a huge decision for your financial future. You can decide if you want to continue grinding and building more wealth at an exponential rate or if you want to taste and sample some of the finer things in life that you have been neglecting up to this point.

If you want to experience the finer things in life, please read the next chapter. If you choose to skip taking a break from the 16-step plan to acquire some expensive toys, skip the next chapter as it doesn't contain any information relevant to becoming financially free or independent.

Real Estate Net Worth and Passive Income at Age 40, 50, and 65

Age	# of Rental Properties	Real Estate Passive Income monthly	Real Estate Net worth
40	3	2400	$400,000
50	9	7200	$1.2 million
65	30	24000	$ 5 million

If you're interested in how much real-estate that I will have at the ages of 40, 50, and 65, please see the graph above. Please note that this example in the table is assuming a house with a worth of $130,000 with an 800 passive rental income stream after expenses.By the age of 40, I would have reached financial freedom and would have at least $2400 dollars coming in per month. At age 50, I would have approximately nine rental properties with at least $7200 dollars coming in per month. At age 65, I would have approximately 30 rental properties with a passive income stream of $24,000 per month. I would have a real estate net worth of at least $5 million dollars. This combined with my other investments would give me an approximate net worth of at least $13 million dollars.

OPTIONAL SECTION
TIME TO CATCH UP TO THE JONESES WITH THEIR BROKE ASS

Now that you're financially independent, it's time to finally acquire some expensive unnecessary luxuries like getting a nicer house, nicer car, and/or any other expensive toys that you have fantasized about. The difference between us acquiring these expensive unnecessary luxuries and how most Americans acquire them will be fundamentally different. We will not go into debt to obtain these expensive luxuries under any means necessary because that defeats the purpose of us learning how to get out and stay out of debt. The proper way to go about financing this new car that you want is to increase how much you're saving for car repairs and/or money towards a new car. Every month, save the total car cost that you want to purchase divided by the number of months that you can wait before you feel like you need the car. I want to repeat that you should never get a car loan to pay for a car, as that is an unnecessary luxury; the car should be paid in cash.

For example, if you wanted to buy a used Dodge Charger that costs 20k, you would save two grand every month to pay for that nice car cash in 10 months. I also want to state that now that we are now financially independent, that does not mean that we are going to be dumb with money and buy tons of unnecessary things. This section is to acquire one or two expensive unnecessary luxuries that you have wanted for a long time and that you deserve for reaching financial independence. You will still stay on the budget that we created in a previous chapter and not go into debt acquiring these new toys. You can stop investing temporarily to acquire these luxuries relatively quickly.

At the time that you are acquiring the things that the Joneses pretended to have, but went into deep debt to obtain, the Joneses' fancy expensive cars are getting reposed, and the expensive house that they had is getting foreclosed by the bank. This is the difference between acquiring these luxuries the correct way by not going into debt to obtain them, and the "American" way of going into debt to pretend that you can afford them when you cannot.

At this point in time, I assume that you are now married with kids or have kids on the way and the 3-bedroom two-bathroom house is starting to get crowded. If you plan on getting a bigger house, I suggest getting a house no more than three times what you initially bought your starter home for. For example, if you bought your starter home for $130,000, you should not buy a house worth more than $390,000. This should be plenty of house for you and any family. As your self-appointed financial advisor, I must inform you that building a swimming pool, if your current property doesn't have one, is a terrible ass investment, because the property value would go up a fraction of what you paid to get the swimming pool created and installed. When it comes to the newer home, we will still save for a 10-20% down payment on this house, get a 10-year mortgage, and make double payments. You will be able to make at least 1.5x payments on this house, because you should at least have $2500 passive income coming in once you move into this house. This goes without saying you should rent out the starter home that you were living in once you move into the new house.

For example, your mortgage payment would be: $2700 dollars a month for a $390,000- house, which should be attainable, because you should be accustomed to budgeting at least $1900 monthly for your starter home and rental properties. You have been budgeting this $1900 monthly for the last 10ish years of your life. The $2700 a month should not be an issue at this point because you should at least be getting paid 45% more than when we started our journey to financial freedom and financial independence. You will also be using the $2400 worth of passive income generated from your three rental properties to make double payments. I just want to state that if you're going to move into a bigger house or get a bigger car, you obviously cannot afford to quit your day/corporate job yet, because your passive income that you were planning to live off is not going towards paying for that bigger house or nicer car.

REPEAT STEPS 10 AND 13 UNTIL YOU BECOME FINANCIALLY FREE

This is the section that will take you from being financially independent to being financially free. Remember from our earlier definitions of both terms, financial independence is where you have more passive income coming in monthly than you have monthly expenses. Even though you have reached financial independence and you technically no longer are required to work a day job to survive, you are still restrained to follow a budget and must live relatively modest. Financial freedom means you have at least a three-million-dollar net worth, and you have enough monthly passive income coming in to replace your corporate/day job's salary.

To achieve this, you will continue steps 11 and 14 of this guide towards financial freedom and financial independence until you have enough passive income coming in to replace your day job. As a refresher, Steps 11 and Steps 14 are investing at least 15-20% of your income into your investment portfolio and acquiring more rental-properties to generate more monthly passive income. This means you will continue investing at least 15% of your income before taxes, and you will continue to acquire more and more rental properties, until you can replace your day job with passive income from your investments, rental properties, and businesses.

If you haven't noticed, I have not once referenced a second income coming into your household. I just want to state that if using this plan, you can become financially independent within 15 years. Imagine the potential wealth and passive income that can be generated off two incomes.

CHAPTER 2
PATH TO FINANCIAL FREEDOM

Now that you have achieved financial independence, I want to expand and go more in depth into the exact differences between financial freedom and financial independence. This is my definition of financial independence and financial freedom, and my definition may not be the same as someone else's.

Criteria	Financial Independence	Financial Freedom
Monthly Passive Income	At least $1600	At least $8000
Net Worth	500 thousand	3 million dollar net worth
Mortgage?	N	N
What comfort level the passive income provides	Enough to cover your monthly expenses with passive income	Enough to cover your monthly paychecks from your day job with passive income
The number of vacations you can take per year	One annually if you budget correctly	You can afford to take a monthly vacation
Availability to deviate from your budget?	N	Y

There are multiple variations of how to go about achieving financial freedom. The strategy that I will continue to and have talked about is the real estate train. To quickly summarize what I have stated in a previous chapter, it's the concept of putting every penny of your rental property income plus your normal double payments budget allocation to continually buy more rental properties to generate more passive income. The time it will take to acquire a new rental property will decrease with every new acquisition of a rental property. Following this strategy, you will eventually get to the point where you have 10 rental properties which would provide $8000 worth of monthly passive income.

The second way to achieve financial freedom is through opening your own business and generating around $8000 of monthly profit through sales. The most realistic option above is a combination between the two above mentioned strategies to achieve financial independence and freedom.

You're probably wondering why I am not including dividends generated by our stocks and bonds, and this is because we will be reinvesting the dividends from our stock and bonds to generate even more passive income from our dividends later. Achieving financial freedom will take some time, dedication, sweat, blood, and tears. I don't even have to tell you or remind you that you can obtain financial freedom, because you already know that you can, because you were dedicated enough to reach the status of financial independence. You have already beaten the statistical odds against you to become financially independent, so continue to defy the odds and continue your journey towards becoming financially free.

I already know a decent group of you is probably wondering why I haven't included social security as a means of passive income in this book. It is because I don't believe that social security is a sustainable program and will be around by the age that you retire. The United States government spends 40% more on social security than the government collects in taxes for social security. The United States cannot continue to keep up with these lopsided payments and it will eventually collapse. Unfortunately, you should not expect social security to be there when you retire, which is why I have not mentioned it as a potential passive income stream up to this point.

CHAPTER 3
SIDE HUSTLES

This section is for anyone who wants to make more money to obtain financial independence, freedom, or get out of debt quicker. There is zero shame in having or getting a side hustle; not only does it give you more cash to achieve your financial goals quicker, it can also be used to increase the quality of your life by increasing the allocated budget for certain sections of your budget. I would recommend obtaining and working a side hustle that you personally enjoy doing because unless you really like your side hustle, you will lack the motivation to work it as well as a forty-hour day job.

People typically find that once they get out of debt or they get a substantial promotion at work, the need to work a side hustle disappears. If you are in a terrible financial situation, you may need to get a side hustle out of necessity, but just remember the necessity of having a side hustle will only last for a couple of years until you get in a better financial situation.

If you have a girlfriend or boyfriend with a lot of "wants" and desires, what I recommend instead is working a side hustle and using a portion of the money generated from that to satisfy their "wants" and their needs or implement the much easier way of getting rid of this needy person. Now that I've talked about why you might want or need a side hustle, let's start discussing some side hustles that I would personally recommend. These are the only side hustles that I have some experience with, or I know someone who has experience in the field, or I know you can get close to $25 an hour doing. If none of these side hustles interest you, there is a list of potential side hustles that you can do provided below in the link.

Link to 99 potential side hustles: https://www.sidehustlenation.com/ideas/

FREELANCING

Freelancing is the concept of taking a skill or sharing knowledge on a subject and getting paid for it. For example, if you're an awesome writer, you can write a blog or article for someone who doesn't like to write and get paid for it. Freelancing can include just about any skill that someone would pay you for. A couple of examples are: web designing, teaching someone a skill such as playing an instrument, consulting someone or a business that you are knowledgeable about, etc. There are plenty of sites that are used by freelancers to get their skills out to as many people as possible. Some of the websites I endorse will be provided below.

Links to good Freelancing Sites: Fiverr: https://www.fiverr.com/, Upwork: https://www.upwork.com/ and Cloud peeps: https://www.cloudpeeps.com/

WORK MORE HOURS

Why does it seem like the least sexy options are always the ones that turn out to typically be the best options? If you have been following this guide, you have a job that pays at least 50k a year so you're getting paid at least $25 dollars an hour. Unless you can beat $25 an hour doing another one of these side hustles financially, it makes the most sense just to work as many hours as humanly possible without losing your sanity. It's also a great way for your boss to notice your hard work. It is also a fact that people who typically work more learn quicker than people who don't, which can translate into you getting promoted quicker than someone who is only working 40 hours a week.

UBERING/LYFT

Being an Uber and Lyft driver can be extremely lucrative if done correctly. If you don't follow the below guide that I will link, I do not recommend driving for Lyft or Uber, because there are so many unforeseen costs that are associated with the job. These unforeseen costs can get so bad that some of these drivers are getting the equivalent of around $4 an hour. Surge pricing (Uber) or Prime Time (Lyft) are times when the demand for rides go up, and supply of drivers goes down, meaning that the rate charged for a ride increases. Taking advantage of these times can lead to the potential for higher earnings for drivers.

You'll see varying opinions on this. Some say that surge and prime time end up wasting your time, as the flood of responding drivers make it even harder to find riders. Some say to take advantage of it if it's occurring in the area you are already driving. The best thing you can do is try it out a few times and see if it works for you. Please read the below guide on how to use Uber and Lyft correctly.

https://www.ridester.com/maximize-uber-earnings/

FLIPPER

I've personally used this side hustle to help pay for college when hard times hit me during my senior year. There is a learning curve when it comes to being a flipper, but once you know how to list things correctly, buy things at the correct price, ship things cost effectively, and how to run an eBay or Amazon store correctly, it can be extremely lucrative. The concept of being a flipper is buying things at a low price and reselling it at a higher price. The standard ways of selling goods are through Amazon, eBay, FacebookMarketplace, and craigslist. You'll have to learn what items to buy, which items are going to sell, and at what price to buy them for. I, at one point, was generating an additional

10k a year flipping. I, however, did not have a passion for it anymore and couldn't force myself to continue flipping.

If you're interested in learning more about being a flipper and want to learn what items to buy and from where to buy them, please check out the Rockstareflipper's YouTube guide to becoming a flipper. It's a very well-directed series that explains the majority of what you'll need to know to become a successful flipper.

Link to RockStarflippers YouTube guide is below:

https://www.youtube.com/watch?v=Xc4OjVDFmyA&list=PLofXh8bXBtpWYTGHSP0iAxVQD9icXD7v6

VENDING MACHINE BUSINESS

I am currently trying to get into the vending machine business because it can eventually turn into a passive income stream once you have enough machines. You see vending machines everywhere, right? You ever thought about owning your own vending machine? To be honest, the hardest part of starting a vending machine business is that it has a higher upfront cost compared to the rest of the side hustles but has some of the highest potential upside with the possibility of eventually becoming passive income. Vending machines can cost anywhere from $500-$1000 for a working used machine in good condition.

I recommend getting a membership to Costco or Sam's Club to buy snacks for your machines stock to keep your profit per item sold high. The expected monthly return on a vending machine can be anywhere from $30-100 dollars a month; it purely depends on the location of the vending machine. Honestly, the hardest part of a vending machine business is convincing a store owner to allow you to put a vending machine in their location. You may have to give up 10% of your profits to that store to convince them to allow you to place your machine in their store.

Please use the below YouTuber as a reference for vending machine:

Link to Vending Machine Guide:
https://www.youtube.com/watch?v=Saqk1kfhJBE

CONTENT CREATOR

A content creator is someone who creates music, videos, or any other form of entertainment. I found that you must be extremely passionate about content creation in order to get to a point of creating a revenue source. If you think you're extremely interesting or you are an expert on a subject, start a YouTube channel and become a content creator. Please be advised, if you start a YouTube channel, that it can take a long time to gain a substantial following. The potential upside of content creation is extremely high, because it can become a source of passive income.

Making music incorporates many of the same concepts of what I have discussed above. Remember, to become a successful content creator you must stay consistent and constantly believe in yourself and don't get discouraged at your current lack of audience. Even if you were to average ten views per video, treat those 10 people like they were a crowd of 10 million. If you're interested on how to become a successful content creator, find your favorite YouTube personality and/or music artist, watch their interview, and take notes on what they did to become famous and implement what you have learned from it.

HAIR SALON/ DOING HAIR

If you have a skill or love of doing hair, start a small business and charge your friends and family and acquaintances to do their hair. This way, you can hang out with your friends, family, or acquaintances while making some money on the side. I know plenty of people who would pay to get their hair done for a fraction of the cost of what a hair salon charges. Why wouldn't they want to save money and get the same quality hair style as a salon for a fraction of the price? There is not a guide that I'm familiar with on doing hair, but you really shouldn't need an in depth guide on how to start charging your acquaintances to do their hair.

ACTING AS AN EXTRA

Please only do this side hustle if you're passionate about acting or your dream is to become an actor. My brother is a grip in the movie business and he says the life of an extra is terrible. You stand around for up to 12 hours a day to, if you're lucky, get 5 seconds of work on a given day. The typical amount of money that you get daily is $50 dollars. Shout out to my Brother Russ for giving me the low-down on the life of an extra.

CHAPTER 4
X FACTOR/OWNING YOUR OWN BUSINESS/INTERVIEW WITH BUSINESS OWNERS

Before I dive into the principles, difficulties, and rewards of owning your own business, I want to talk about the concept of what an X factor is. If you've ever watched wrestling, this is like a wrestler's signature move that he or she would pull out to finish off his opponent. Instead of using your X factor to wrestle and fight people, the X factor is going to be your signature move when fighting for your financial freedom. If you're following this guide, you will be putting 6.5% of your investment portfolio allocation towards working on yourself and your business.

If you haven't found what your passion is yet, spend this 6.5% trying out everything that you ever wanted to try before to see what you're truly passionate about. Once you find your calling or passion in life, start investing in equipment, knowledge, and/or tools that you'll need to start your business. An example of this would be, if I'm truly passionate about photography, I would go out and buy a camera with the 6.5% allocation for investing in myself.

Please don't get discouraged when you're making little to no income during the early stages of your business. Remember that over time, your business will grow and eventually start making you money, and besides we're not counting on this income to be financially free or independent anyway. Any income you make off your X factor should be considered a major win. Just think about how amazing it is that you're working for yourself and making money doing something that you would do for free anyway. Instead of going into depth about how you should open your own business and the dedication that it takes in order to make a business successful, I would rather provide you with a couple of stories of people who have achieved financial freedom and independence through owning their own businesses.

I, honestly, think reading these people's stories about how they opened their businesses, will be better because you will learn their struggles, what they wish they would have done sooner or better, advice for people starting out, and general tips that someone who hasn't experienced it could never provide. I interviewed two different business owners that have different businesses and different experiences to give the stories some variety. Before we look at the stories, I just want to state that yes owning and managing a business is a lot of work, but there is no better feeling than owning your own business. It is important to understand that one day, your X Factor can become your biggest source of passive income.

Below are two interviews of self-made millionaires who own their own businesses. It's almost eerie how similar their opinions on money are to the principles of this book. I just want to state that I did not edit any of their stories, opinions on money, or how they successfully opened a business, the answers they replied with are 100% genuine, below

Synopsis of Jamaican Restaurant Owner's INTERVIEW

He states that it takes plenty of hard work and dedication to open a business; people think that owning a business requires a lot of luck, but it's all about the preparation to become wealthy. It's all about how you save and invest your money. People get tied down in credit card debt, and he suggests that you don't run up debt. People are in love with the concept of spending money especially in America. People get trapped in the American dream of having fun and not having enough time to focus and do the hard work it requires to become wealthy and successfully open a business. His dad taught him to save money and to properly have a relationship with money. He learned to save and invest even way back when he was in Jamaica.

He originally migrated from Jamaica and started buying as much real estate as possible to rent out and generate passive income. After seven years of working for corporate America, he bought his first rental property. He avoided all credit cards like the plague, because he didn't want to be in debt. He started investing his money at an extremely early age in real estate to start generating passive income. He lived in a duplex and had the other person's rent pay for the mortgage. He lived five years mortgage-free in this duplex, due to his tenant paying the mortgage. He has kept all his rental properties after he paid them off. He lived in his family's house for 10 years to save cash to be able to invest. He did a rent-to-own for the properties, but he eventually sold them.

He believes that 401ks are crucial and that you should always do the matching programs that these companies offer. He always knew that he wanted to own a business and his wife always wanted to have a restaurant. She was always passionate about cooking, so once he got the opportunity, he opened a restaurant. He believes the main ingredient to owning a successful business is research. He loves owning a business because he can set his own hours. He believes that you must be sensible about how you spend your money and that you should always weigh your wants versus your needs. His house is paid off, and he paid off his rental property. His business is paid off. He says that he accomplished this by years of common sense and discipline and that he never splurged like the average American. He never allowed conveniences to become overindulgence. As I was interested in how he started his business, I asked him a couple of direct questions. The questions I asked and the response that I received are below:

What was your biggest challenge of opening your business?

Being a minority was the biggest challenge for him to open a business. Depending on where you live, some people will have open arms if you want to open a business, and with some people, you must push their arms open. Fayetteville has the vast majority of predominantly white-owned businesses. People in power can try to stop you from opening your own business, but you can't let them stop you. You might have to work a little harder to get their help or trust, but it can be done.

What would you say to someone who wants to open their own business?

Always have a six months nest egg in your account. If you plan to open a business, increase your nest egg to cover any expenses for at least a year. Even if you were to go the route of buying the right to open a franchise, it can still take some time to get some brand recognition. You want to make sure you can survive rough months as to why you are increasing your nest egg allocation. There will be plenty of rough days and you must have the capital to cover all expenses. Decide what your passion is and create a business that you are passionate about. If you have passion and dedication, you can make it happen

What steps did you take to open a business?

I started by doing tons of research on the business that I wanted to open. I would say narrow your passions down to three things that you are passionate about. Do your research on three businesses out of the many. Narrow down your three choices by the amount of investment capital it would take, potential profit, finding something that you feel comfortable doing, and making sure that your wife or husband is supportive of your dream. Look at the viability of your business in your area, demand, and potential profitability of this business.

Any Additional tips that someone should know about owning a business?

That brand power is critical, look at how you market your brand and find ways that you can improve on that. Some ways you can do that is by keeping your ratings up on online rating sites and apps, and making your customers feel valued. Always keep growing as a business and never be content with where your business is. Remember that you can always improve some aspect of your business.

HENRY AND JULIET

What should you look for when looking to open a business?

You look for a niche in a marketplace, something that currently isn't being fulfilled. Find something. The idea can be complicated or simple; sometimes it can be so simple that nobody's done it.

What steps did you take to make sure your business was a success?

They got people who were advertising in local newspapers, and they educated them on how they can get more business online from Google. They advertised websites, so they created a directory of businesses from the newspapers, created websites to advertise for and to them.

What challenges did you face with your business?

The concept of having a website for your business 15 years ago was not as mainstream as it is now, during business meetings with potential customers, they must convince people that it could increase sales in their businesses.

What was the turning point of your business?

They found commercial success on a big platform, after they made a Jewish man's business go from being worth 1 million to 3 million after a year. He told his community, and it opened the door to work with the

Jewish community. In order to cater to their culture, Juliet dressed in a certain way that matched their culture, in order to show respect. Even though Henry was the CEO and founder of their business vision, he was typically absent from this discussion, because just the fact that he had a darker skin color could potentially lose him the deal. Please keep in mind ago that this was twenty years ago, and people were not as tolerate as they are now. They eventually landed bigger names such as Tesc. The company that Juliet and Henry own Vision increased the profitability of Tesc's ICO by over 50%.

How do you handle the financials of your business?

They wanted to stay debt-free with their business and never use a line of credit to pay for anything. Henry would save money every single day. He started to put 50 dollars from his business into 4 accounts.He suggests starting with 10 dollars a day to save money. Always prepare for tax season with your business, to do this put 30% revenue away for your business, and if there is a surplus, you put it into your savings account. A lot of people fail because they can't pay their taxes. Always have four bank accounts, one for your business taxes, interme- diate savings (monthly expenses), and cash savings (daily expenses and transactions), and one you don't take money out from.

What are some general business tips for people looking to start up a business?

Never do a job or start work for a client without a deposit or payment first. If someone is being cheap and you have issues getting money from them, never do business with them again after the initial time. You're better off having five good clients that you don't have issues with, than 20 bad clients who are not loyal, rude, and extremely cheap. Always consider the cost of the work and how much profit you will make in the deal and weigh the options to see if the job is worth it. Always prepare and have a plan for the worst-case scenario and ensure that you have enough money in reserve to cover all your potential costs. Make sure every week that your business is in the black and keep up with any revenue with excel. Make sure you know your cash flow coming in and going out. Talk to your clients very regularly, even if it's a phone call about nothing. Make affordable packages that people can afford, such as $29 a week for a business compared to $1700 a year.

How did you get started with your real estate business?

The original house where they raised their son shot up in value due to the location becoming extremely desirable. They took the money from that and bought another property to live in and used some newly acquired inheritance money to start looking for new rental properties. They had a premonition that a new cross rail system was going to be built in the poorest area in London. They started looking in this area by looking at ten properties. This was in order to guarantee that they did their due diligence to make sure they were getting the best possible deal on a rental property in this area.

After finding a suitable rental property, they put about 50k in total towards this house through the cost to buy it and the repair and maintenance cost. They more than doubled their money in a couple years once the cross rail system was built.

What is your most profitable rental property that you own?

They acquired a three-story Victorian house that they turned into an HMO; if you don't know what an HMO is, it's a rental room-based house. There are a couple of stipulations when it comes to an HMO, you must supply all appliances such as the microwave, stove, washer, dryer and etc. Traditionally with an HMO, all bills are included in the renter's monthly fee for staying there. Additional stipulations with an HMO are that you are required to meet certain rules and standards. For starters, they must be accredited, and keep the home in pristine condition, and must do weekly safety checkup to make sure the house is passing all rules and regulations. Juliet and Henry say even with all the above stipulations it is still worth it, because they are essentially getting 5x the normal amount of rent if they were to rent the house out to one family.

Tips for Rental Property Management and Rental Property Investors

Be selective with your potential tenants; don't just try to fit a renter into your house, properly screen them to make sure that they would take care of your house. Through experience, tenants that work in technology and medical field are the best, because they work all the time. Don't be afraid of buying a property that requires some work; remember that you must take some risk when it comes to investing.

Now that we have read the stories and advise that these two millionaires have provided, I briefly want to discuss the difference between a franchise and a non-franchise business. A franchise is the concept of buying the right to open a store by an established company, an example of a franchise would be a McDonalds. A non-franchise business is where the business is completely new and comes with no name recognition like a franchise would provide.

If you are interested in obtaining a potential franchise, I have provided below is a list of advantages and disadvantages of buying and owning a franchise:

Advantages of buying a franchise

- Franchises offer the independence of small business ownership supported by the benefits of a big business network.
- You don't necessarily need business experience to run a franchise. Franchisors usually provide the training you need to operate their business model.

- Franchises have a higher rate of success than start-up businesses.
- You may find it easier to secure finance for a franchise. It may cost less to buy a franchise than start your own business of the same type.
- Franchises often have an established reputation and image, proven management and work practices, access to national advertising, and ongoing support.

Disadvantages of buying a franchise

- Buying a franchise means entering into a formal agreement with your franchisor.
- Franchise agreements dictate how you run the business, so there may be little room for creativity.
- There are usually restrictions on where you operate, the products you sell, and the suppliers you use.
- Bad performances by other franchisees may affect your franchise's reputation.
- Buying a franchise means ongoing sharing of profit with the franchisor.
- Franchisors do not have to renew an agreement at the end of the franchise term.

Once you've started making money with your business, it's time to make it official by registering with your state and government to reap those sweet business tax breaks. It's time to officially go get your business license! I will link a guide below that explains how to go about getting your business license so that you can legally own a business in your state. I just want to state that you may need special permissions depending on the business that you have decided to start.

A link on how to obtain a business license is below:

https://www.wikihow.com/Obtain-a-Business-License

A link to find what permits you need for your business is below:

https://www.sba.gov/business-guide/launch-your-business/apply-licenses-permits

CHAPTER 5
FINANCIAL/MONEY SAVING TIPS

HEALTH INSURANCE

Health Insurance is a mandatory necessity that everyone needs, but I can almost assuredly tell you that you are overpaying for your health insurance. If you're like me and you take care of yourself and live a healthy lifestyle, you should consider getting a high deductible health insurance plan. People who live healthy lifestyles rarely get sick, and if you do get sick, the money you're saving on your monthly health insurance bill will more than make up the high deductible that you will have to pay. If you've been following this guide, you should have up to 10-20k in your bank account for a rainy-day fund and be allocating $50-100 to your HSA each month in case you go to the doctor and need to pay the high deductible.

There're three categories that people who need health insurance fall into. If you're a young healthy adult that rarely gets sick, you should strongly consider getting the highest deductible health plan possible and put 50-$100 every month towards an HSA. An HSA is a health savings account that is pre and post-tax free if you use its contents for health-related purposes. If you were to put $100 dollars monthly into an HSA, it would effectively only cost you around $75 dollars to put $100 dollars in the HSA due to the tax benefits of the HSA. Another benefit of the HSA is that many of them provide the capability to be put in investing accounts to have them grow tax-free. Obviously, if you ever use the HSA for anything else besides health care, you'll have to pay your federal taxes and any capital gains tax that you may have accrued over the span of its growth of the HSA. A high deductible health insurance plan typically ends up being the cheapest option to cover yourself with health insurance.

The second category of health insurance is typically for people who have serious medical conditions that require them to make frequent trips to the doctor. This type of people end up hitting and paying off the limit of their deductible liability every year. In this case, it makes more sense to upgrade your healthcare plan to have a lower annual deductible but higher monthly payments. If you have kids and a wife and your health insurance would cover them, it also makes sense to get a better healthcare plan, because kids can and will get sick frequently and you don't ever want to be in the position where you can't afford to properly take care of your kids. If you have any more questions about what is the best health insurance plan for you, please reference and read the below guide for more information.

Guide to health insurance: https://www.nerdwallet.com/blog/health/health-insurance-guide/

LIFE INSURANCE

Before we delve deep into the conversation of what the best life insurance plan is for you, I want to state the difference between term life insurance and whole life insurance. Term life insurance covers you only for a time; this time typically lasts 15-25 years and after the term of the policy, you can keep the policy, but only by paying a ludicrous amount of money. I don't recommend keeping your term life insurance policy after the initial term has expired, because it is no longer an effective way to protect yourself from an early demise.

Whole life insurance, like it states in the title, lasts your whole life and you are given a fixed rate that you pay monthly. Whole life insurance guarantees your family will receive the face value of the policy when you die. You can get a lot more coverage for a cheaper monthly price with a term life insurance policy when compared to a whole life insurance policy. The reason why term life policy providers can do this is because chances are that you are not going to die in your 20s, 30s, or 40s are extremely low, but this is when you would want a term life policy. This, in turn, allows them to be able to pay more money out in the event of your untimely death during the term of the policy, because if you don't die during the policy's term that don't have to pay anything.

The fact that you won't get anything if you don't suffer a untimely death is a non-issue, because we are not looking at getting an insurance policy as means of an investment, but as a backup plan in case of a terrible untimely death. You wouldn't want to leave your family without some money to take care of themselves while you are building up your fortune during the earlier part of your life. Whole life insurance guarantees to give you money when you die, but it'll have a much higher monthly principal and much lower face value when compared to term life insurance. The only situation where getting a whole life insurance policy would be better than a term life insurance policy would be when you are bad at handling money and you are not financially literate. Whole life insurance, in this situation, is a failsafe to make sure this type of person has at least enough money to bury themselves.

I only recommend getting a term life insurance policy when you are still building wealth, and you may be at risk of leaving your wife and kids in a terrible financial situation if you were to die untimely. An example of when you might want to get a term life insurance policy is when you are 25 years of age with your wife and kids solely dependent on your income. If you plan to get term life insurance, you should get at least twice your salary for the face value of the term life insurance policy. Once you reach financial freedom and independence, you have no need for any type of life insurance, since your family has more passive income coming in than they have expenses and you have 10-20k in your money market account that can go towards your burial.

I already know that a lot of people are probably thinking whole life insurance policies are better because with them, at least, one is guaranteed some type of return on money for their family when they die, but with term life insurance policies, one will more than likely get nothing! Technically, what you are thinking is true, but I can almost guarantee you that the money that your family would receive from that whole life insurance policy would be less than half of the money that you paid in monthly payments.

Let's think about whole life insurance policies logically. If whole life insurance policies were actually worth a damn as an investment and were monetarily beneficial to its customers, every single life insurance company would go bankrupt, because none of them would be profitable. If you were to save the monthly principal of a whole life insurance policy in a Roth IRA or 401k for 20 years, which do you think would contain more money? Your 10,000-face value whole life insurance policy or a 401k/Roth IRA that averages a 10% annual return on your money?

HOME INSURANCE

Below are twelve steps to help guarantee that you will get the best price for your home insurance:

1. Shop around.

It'll take some time but could save you a good sum of money. Ask your friends, check the Yellow Pages, or contact your state insurance department. National Association of Insurance Commissioners (www.naic.org) has information to help you choose an insurer in your state, including complaints. States often make information available on typical rates charged by major insurers and many states provide the frequency of consumer complaints by company.

Also check consumer guides, insurance agents, companies, and online insurance quote services. This will give you an idea of price ranges and tell you which companies have the lowest prices. But don't consider price alone. The insurer you select should offer a fair price and deliver the quality service you would expect if you needed assistance in filing a claim.

So in assessing service quality, use the complaint information cited above and talk to a number of insurers to get a feeling for the type of service they give. Ask them what they would do to lower your costs.

Check the financial stability of the companies you are considering with rating companies such as A.M. Best (www.ambest.com) and Standard & Poor's (www.standardandpoors.com/ratings) and consult consumer magazines. When you've narrowed the field to three insurers, get price quotes.

2. **Raise your deductible.**

Deductibles are the amount of money you have to pay toward a loss before your insurance company starts to pay a claim, according to the terms of your policy. The higher your deductible, the more money you can save on your premiums. Nowadays, most insurance companies recommend a deductible of at least $500. If you can afford to raise your deductible to $1,000, you may save as much as 25 percent. Remember, if you live in a disaster-prone area, your insurance policy may have a separate deductible for certain kinds of damage; if you live near the coast in the East, you may have a separate windstorm deductible; if you live in a state vulnerable to hail storms, you may have a separate deductible for hail; and if you live in an earthquake-prone area, your earthquake policy has a deductible.

3. **Don't confuse what you paid for your house with rebuilding costs.**

The land under your house isn't at risk from theft, windstorm, fire, and the other perils covered in your homeowner's policy. So don't include its value in deciding how much homeowners insurance to buy. If you do, you will pay a higher premium than you should.

4. **Buy your home and auto policies from the same insurer.**

Some companies that sell homeowners, auto and liability coverage will take 5 to 15 percent off your premium if you buy two or more policies from them. But make certain this combined price is lower than buying the different coverages from different companies.

5. **Make your home more disaster resistant.**

Find out from your insurance agent or company representative what steps you can take to make your home more resistant to windstorms and other natural disasters. You may be able to save on your premiums by adding storm shutters, reinforcing your roof, or buying stronger roofing materials. Older homes can be retrofitted to make them better able to withstand earthquakes. In addition, consider modernizing your heating, plumbing, and electrical systems to reduce the risk of fire and water damage.

6. **Improve your home security.**

You can usually get discounts of at least 5 percent for a smoke detector, burglar alarm, or dead-bolt locks. Some companies offer to cut your premium by as much as 15 or 20 percent if you install a sophisticated sprinkler system and a fire and burglar alarm that rings at the police, fire, or other monitoring stations. These systems aren't cheap and not every system qualifies for a discount. Before you buy such a system, find out what kind your insurer recommends, how much the device would cost, and how much you'd save on premiums.

7. Seek out other discounts.

Companies offer several types of discounts, but they don't all offer the same discount or the same amount of discount in all states. For example, since retired people stay at home more than working people, they are less likely to be burglarized and may spot fires sooner, too. Retired people also have more time for maintaining their homes. If you're at least 55 years old and retired, you may qualify for a discount of up to 10 percent at some companies. Some employers and professional associations administer group insurance programs that may offer a better deal than you can get elsewhere.

8. Maintain a good credit record.

Establishing a solid credit history can cut your insurance costs. Insurers are increasingly using credit information to price homeowners insurance policies. In most states, your insurer must advise you of any adverse action, such as a higher rate, at which time you should verify the accuracy of the information on which the insurer relied. To protect your credit standing, pay your bills on time, don't obtain more credit than you need and keep your credit balances as low as possible. Check your credit record on a regular basis and have any errors corrected promptly so that your record remains accurate.

9. Stay with the same insurer.

If you've kept your coverage with a company for several years, you may receive a special discount for being a long-term policyholder. Some insurers will reduce their premiums by 5 percent if you stay with them for three to five years and by 10 percent if you remain a policyholder for six years or more. But make certain to periodically compare this price with that of other policies.

10. Review the limits in your policy and the value of your possessions at least once a year.

You want your policy to cover any major purchases or additions to your home. But you don't want to spend money for coverage you don't need. If your five-year-old fur coat is no longer worth the $5,000 you paid for it, you'll want to reduce or cancel your floater (extra insurance for items whose full value is not covered by standard homeowners policies such as expensive jewelry, high-end computers, and valuable art work) and pocket the difference.

11. Look for private insurance if you are in a government plan.

If you live in a high-risk area -- say, one that is especially vulnerable to coastal storms, fires, or crime -- and have been buying your homeowners insurance through a government plan, you should check with an insurance agent or company representative or contact your state department of insurance for the names of companies that might be interested in your business. You may find that there are steps you can take that would allow you to buy insurance at a lower price in the private market.

12. When you're buying a home, consider the cost of homeowners insurance

You may pay less for insurance if you buy a house close to a fire hydrant or in a community that has a professional rather than a volunteer fire department. It may also be cheaper if your home's electrical, heating, and plumbing systems are less than 10 years old. If you live in the East, consider a brick home because it's more wind resistant. If you live in an earthquake-prone area, look for a wooden frame house because it is more likely to withstand this type of disaster. Choosing wisely could cut your premiums by 5 to 15 percent.

Check the CLUE (Comprehensive Loss Underwriting Exchange) report of the home you are thinking of buying. These reports contain the insurance claim history of the property and can help you judge some of the problems the house may have.

AUTO INSURANCE

Below is an eight-step guide to making sure that you have the best possible price for your auto insurance.

1. Don't assume any one company is the cheapest

Some companies spend a lot of money on commercials to convince you they offer the lowest car insurance rates. But no single insurer is the low-price leader for everyone. The insurance company that's cheapest for one person in one place might be the most expensive option for a driver in a different state.

The only way to ensure you're getting the lowest rate possible is to shop around.

A NerdWallet analysis of rates shows why shopping around is so important. Here are some of the rates we found for a 40-year-old driver with good credit and a clean driving record, buying a full coverage policy:

- In Alabama, Allstate would charge $1,287 a year, on average — the cheapest rate in the state for a driver without a military connection. Geico's average rate is $487 higher.
- In Oregon, it's the opposite: Geico is cheapest, with an average rate of $1,221, and Allstate's average is $729 higher.

- Esurance is the cheapest option for California drivers at $1,196, on average, but in New York, it's the most expensive at $3,544.

2. Don't ignore local and regional insurers

Just four companies — <u>Allstate, Geico, Progressive and State Farm</u> — control more than half of the nation's auto insurance business. But smaller, regional insurers such as Auto-Owners Insurance and Erie Insurance often have higher customer satisfaction ratings than the big names — and they may have lower car insurance rates, too.

3. Ask about discounts

Insurers provide a variety of discounts, which can mean lower insurance rates for customers who:

- Bundle car insurance with other policies, such as homeowners insurance.
- Insure multiple cars with one policy.
- Have a clean driving record.
- Pay their entire annual or six-month premium at once.
- Agree to receive documents online.
- Own a car with certain anti-theft or safety features.
- Are members of particular professional organizations or affiliate groups.

Don't be swayed, however, by a long list of possible discounts. Compare rates from multiple insurers.

4. Pay your bills on time

Your credit score is a significant factor in the car insurance quotes you receive — except in California, Hawaii, and Massachusetts, which don't allow insurers to consider credit when setting rates. Insurance companies say customers' credit has been shown to correlate with their chances of filing claims.

A NerdWallet analysis found that having poor credit can increase people's car insurance rates by hundreds of dollars a year compared with having good credit. (In most situations, a FICO score of 579 or lower is considered "poor" credit, but insurers have their own credit models that may have a different cutoff.)

Improve your credit — and get lower insurance rates — by paying your bills on time and reducing your debt. Track your progress by checking your credit score regularly.

5. Check insurance costs when buying a car

You probably already pay attention to factors such as fuel efficiency and repair costs when picking a car to buy, but you should also consider insurance premiums. A NerdWallet analysis of the cheapest cars to insure among top-selling vehicles found the lowest insurance rates are for the Subaru Outback, the Jeep Wrangler, and the Honda CR-V.

6. Skip comprehensive and collision coverage for an older car

Collision coverage pays to repair the damage to your vehicle from another car or an object such as a fence. Comprehensive coverage pays to repair vehicle damage from weather, animal crashes, floods, fire, and vandalism. It also covers car theft. But the maximum payout under either policy is limited by the value of the car if it's totaled or stolen. If your car is older and has a low market value, it may not make sense to shell out for these types of coverage.

7. Raise your deductible

If you buy comprehensive and collision coverage, you can save money by opting for higher deductibles. (There is no deductible on liability insurance, which pays for the damage you cause others in an accident.)

8. Consider usage-based or pay-per-mile insurance

If you're a safe driver who doesn't log many miles, consider a usage-based insurance program such as Allstate's Drivewise, Progressive's Snapshot, or State Farm's Drive Safe & Save. By signing up for these programs, you let your insurer track your driving in exchange for possible discounts based on how much you drive, when you drive, and how well you drive.

SOCIAL SECURITY AND MEDICARE

If you're already in your 50s, there's a decent chance that social security and Medicare may still be around by the time you retire. I'll quickly touch on social security. To maximize your social security, wait as long as humanly possible to start collecting it. Every year that you defer, you increase the size of your monthly checks that are given from social security; this is the traditional advice given by so many financial advisors and I disagree heavily with the previous statement. This mathematically makes sense because you'll get more money this way, but they don't put in context just how unsustainable the concept of social security is. The United States government spends over 40% more on social security than they receive in taxes for social security. The concept of social security can explode any day. At a maximum, I recommend waiting until the bare minimum age requirement without incurring heavy fees for social security.

Let's say that I'm wrong and social security somehow survives, if it does, it will be nothing but a shell of what it was previously. You should not plan on counting on a system that is unsustainable and fundamentally flawed. You need a minimum of 10 years of work history to receive Social Security benefits, except in the case of a non-working spouse of a worker with that type of employment history. Non-working ex-spouses who were married for 10 years or more also qualify based on their former spouse's employment record.

Under the current Social Security system, you can begin to receive benefits at any time beginning at age 62 and ending at age 70. While claiming at age 62 puts income in your bank account at the earliest possible opportunity, that decision comes at a cost.

Figure 1 shows how a benefit of $1,000 a month expected at full retirement age is impacted by claiming early and claiming later. Claiming at age 62 reduces the monthly benefit by 25%, while waiting until age 70 increases the benefit by 32%. There is no benefit to be gained by waiting until after age 70 to claim under the current benefits law.

If you have more questions about social security, the link below contains more information:

https://www.kiplinger.com/article/retirement/T051-C032-S014-5-steps-to-maximize-your-social-security-benefit.html

I'll briefly touch on Medicare, but once again I don't believe it's a sustainable system because the United States government spends more money annually on Medicare than it gets in taxes to pay for it. You start receiving Medicare at age 65. Medicare is made up of four parts: Part A (hospital insurance) helps pay for inpatient hospital stays, stays in skilled nursing facilities, surgery, hospice care, and even some home health care for free. Part B (medical insurance) helps pay for doctors' visits, outpatient care, some preventive services, and some medical equipment and supplies, but there is a monthly premium associated with Part B. Part C comprises Medicare Advantage Plans. Part D also has a monthly premium associated with it, but it covers any drug related coverage.

If you're interested in any insurance plan that isn't mentioned above, please see the link below:

https://www.aarpmedicareplans.com/medicare-education/medicare-supplement-plans.html.

You shouldn't even really need Medicare, unless you are already super close to the age of 65 and you're not yet financially independent or free. If you've been reading this book, you should be financially independent or free and any health costs that come up after the age of 65 should be a non-issue.

If you are interested in more information about Medicare, please read the link below for more information:

https://www.kiplinger.com/slideshow/retirement/T039-S001-7-things-medicare-doesn-t-cover/index.html)

GET LONG-TERM CARE INSURANCE

You're probably asking what Long-Term Care Insurance is and why you need it. **Long Term Care Insurance (LTCI)** is different from traditional health insurance because it is designed to cover your long-term care needs, support, and services when the inevitable impact of aging or acquired disability gets to you. It includes custodial and personal care whenever and wherever you plan to receive care, be it in your own home, nursing facility, or a community organization.

Depending on your preferred insurance company, you can choose from various benefits and care options that will ensure your care whenever and wherever you need it.

The reason why you need Long-Term Car Insurance is because since you may need assistance to function once you become older, the last thing that you want to be is a liability to your family. Nothing is more stressful than having to put your life on hold to take care of a family member that cannot function on their own. The cost of Long-Term Care Insurance varies based on the age you bought the policy; experts suggest the perfect age to get long-term care insurance is in your middle 50s. Your gender, health, and the amount of coverage are all major factors to be considered in figuring out how much your monthly payments will be.

The Daily Benefit amount or how much the insurance company is going to allocate a day towards the cost of someone taking care of you when you need it, the benefit period or how long the benefits of the policy will last, and the inflation protection are all things that will determine the monthly rate, the certification period, or the definite amount of time that an insurance company takes to assess whether you are eligible for long term care and the elimination period or the period that must pass for the beginning of the disability.

As a general pricing guide for long-term insurance, you should not pay more than 2000 to 4000 dollars a year in payments.

The link below finds the best possible prices for long-term care insurance in your area:

https://www.reviews.com/life-insurance/long-term-care/.

If you want more information about long-term care insurance please check out the website below:

https://www.nerdwallet.com/blog/insurance/long-term-care-insurance/

USING A ROUNDING-UP APPLICATION/SERVICE

Every time you swipe your credit card or buy something from your bank account, it rounds up the amount to the nearest dollar and automatically routes the rounded-up portion of the transaction to your savings or money market account. You should ask the companies that you have your credit cards and banks with if they have a rounding up policy or rule for purchases. I promise you that you won't even notice that the rounding policy or rule is in effect and it will help you slowly save money towards your rainy-day fund.

I recommend using the app Qapital, because it automatically does the rounding-up policy or rule for you once you have linked your bank or credit card accounts. I love Qapital because it gives you more customization on how much to round up and exactly where you want the money that it's saving to be placed. In Qapital, there is no real limit to how much you can round up; the setting that I personally use is for every purchase to round up to the nearest dollar amount + $1. This helps me save when I am making bad dietary decisions by buying fast food.

Link to Qapital: https://www.qapital.com/

SOLAR PANELS

Not only are solar panels good for the environment, they also can be good for your wallet as well. I only recommend getting solar panels on a house that you plan on staying in for at least 7.5 years or more, due to the fact that solar panels don't start turning a profit on your initial investment until 7.5 years after they have been initially installed. I also only recommend getting solar panels if you're in a sunny state or semi sunny state, because the amount of sun that the solar panel will receive to convert into energy will be lower if not. Many governments have tax incentives for installing and using solar panels, which results in you getting the solar panel for around 66%-80% of the actual cost. The number of solar panels that you'll need depends on the size of your house and the amount of electricity you use monthly.

If you completely want to be off the grid, many solar panel companies such as Solar City sell products that allow you to store any access energy that your solar panels generate during the day so that it can be used at night. Solar City also sells roofing for your house that doubles as solar panels, in case you need a new roof and/or plan to build a house. This essentially allows you not to have an electrical bill anymore. If you have a large number of solar panels and/or generate more energy than you use, some states will allow you to sell excess power back to the electric company.

Wouldn't it be awesome to get a check from the electric company every month instead of you sending them a check?

Please use the link below as a guide to find out how many solar panels you need and how much it will cost you depending on the percent of your electricity that will be generated by solar panels:

Also, links to calculate how many solar panels you will need as well as the company Solar City are below:

Link to guide on how to sell energy back to your electric company:https://solartechonline.com/blog/net-metering-how-to-sell-residential-solar-power-back-to-the-utility-company/

Link to Solar Panel Calculator:https://news.energysage.com/how-much-does-the-average-solar-panel-installation-cost-in-the-u-s/.

Link to Solar City: https://www.tesla.com/solarpanels?energy_redirect=true.

BE A FINANCIAL NINJA

Ninjas are silent assassins who are formally trained in the art of ninjutsu. The only difference between an actual ninja and a financial ninja is that, number one, we don't kill or assassinate people for obvious reasons, and two instead of being formally trained in the art of ninjutsu, you are trained in the art of finances and investing. Like the ninja, we will be silent during our operations of being a multi-millionaire. The last thing you want after you work your ass off to achieve financial freedom and independence is to be hated on or envied for your newfound wealth.

A financial ninja never talks about how much money they own or how much their net worth is unless it's someone they trust to the upmost degree. If you talk about your wealth frequently or often, you will make yourself a target for haters and even potential robbers or thieves. If someone you know happens to know your well off asks for a loan and you feel obligated to help them because you don't want to lose them over money, give them a copy of this book. And tell them that the knowledge in it is worth more than the money they are asking for.

AVOID PONZI SCHEMES

Ever received an email where it claims that you can have a million dollars easily with no money down? Or the classic email from one person in the world that knows a secret about making money nobody else knows on how to make you a millionaire? Words like fast cash and easy cash, and beating the market, do you know what they all have in common? If they are ever used in a sales pitch to sell you something, there's a 99% chance that it is a scam. After reading this book, you've hopefully realized that's there's no get-rich schemes that works. Avoid anyone who tells you that they can make you rich overnight; they are 100% telling you a lie and want to take your hard-earned money away from you.

You ever heard of the term "social marketing?" It's where they claim you can be your own boss, work your own hours, and be a business owner. Technically, they aren't lying, but would you take this offer if you had a 1% chance of getting a 100k job that you love and where you could be a business owner, but there is a 99% chance you will loss at least 5k, lost half of your friends, and hated your life? You probably wouldn't take that offer, would you?

Well, that's exactly what these social networking businesses are truly offering you. Less than 1% ever make money in social marketing business and I'm not talking about a lot of money either; the equivalent of working a job at McDonalds type of salary. If you are looking for a job that pays 100k, the odds of you succeeding are closer to .1% in social networking businesses. I know these are "actual" business and all that and it's not a pyramid scheme, but if they draw a picture of how you get paid and the hierarchy of how people get paid with social marketing, I'm willing to bet it resembles a pyramid in some shape way or fashion. Avoid social marketing companies; if you're resourceful enough to be successful at these, you will have no problem opening your own business and becoming successful.

MISCELLANEOUS TIPS THAT I IMPLEMENT TO SAVE MONEY

1. Buying store brand food

If you're looking at a way to save money, I recommend buying store brand foods where applicable. You can save yourself $10-30 every time you go to the grocery store by implementing this strategy.

2. Get rid of subscriptions

Ger rid of any subscriptions of things that you are currently not using anymore. Get rid of Netflix, Hulu, Amazon Prime, and any non-necessary subscriptions that you may have. If applicable, get rid of any meal, clothes, or supply delivery programs and please consider doing some shopping instead of paying for a premium for these delivery programs for convenience.

3. Stop smoking and drinking

I don't want to sound like I'm preaching to you, but quitting smoking cigarettes and consuming alcohol in excess can save you a lot of money. You'll be surprised how much you can save by cutting back or quitting these habits. You can easily save $100 a month if you're a heavy smoker or drinker. An additional side effect is that you'll be healthier, so you'll have a better chance to enjoy the financial freedom and independence that you've been working so hard to achieve.

4. Cut out cable, get sling TV instead

If you currently pay for cable and/or any expensive show-based subscriptions, you should consider getting a sling TV subscription, which gives you access to 50 channels for a way lower price when compared to any offer from cable providers.

A link about sling TV is listed below:

Link to Sling TV: https://www.sling.com/

5. Get a programmable thermostat

A programmable thermostat allows you to turn on and off your A/C or heating system, when you're not home. You can automatically set the programmable thermostat to turn on the heat or A/C an hour before you would typically get back from work. Using your A/C and heating system only when you need it can save you hundreds of dollars every year.

These miscellaneous money-saving tips are ones that I implement in my daily life. They can help you save an extra couple hundred dollars monthly that can be used to invest or help pay off debts. If you're a total cheap ass like me, I recommend getting the book, *Pogue's Basics: Money* because this book provides information to teach you how to save money on just about everything. There are literally almost 300 pages of money-saving tips in the book.

Another great resource that you can use for tips about saving money on daily expenses is Clark Howard's website. Clark Howard is an absolute guru when it comes to saving money on every expense. His website is full of hidden gems on how to save money.

The link to his website is below:

https://clark.com/

Link to *Pogue's Basics: Money* is below if you're interested in buying and reading the book:

https://urlzs.com/ygdEy

CHAPTER 6
TAX TIPS

Ever heard a politician or someone say that paying taxes is for the middle class or poor people? Obviously, this is an exaggeration, but with every exaggeration, there is a certain degree of truth behind it. Typically, wealthy individuals are seen as scoundrels because they try and avoid paying as much tax as humanly possible through the use of tax credits, legal tax shelters, tax benefits, and tax laws. The question that I want to propose to you is this: What's stopping you from taking advantage of the same principles that wealthy people do? After reading the tax tips below, you'll also know how to use the same legal tax dodges that the rich use to avoid most of their tax burden.

Listed below is not an exhaustive list of every single tax credit, tax law, tax shelter, tax benefit or loophole. The information is merely a starter point from which you can do research. A lot of the tax laws and benefits will probably not apply to you, due to the fact that you may have too great of an annual income. I just want to state that you will generally pay less taxes filing under the general deduction, rather than filing through itemizing your taxes. As at the time of writing this book in 2019, Congress has passed a bill to increase the general tax deduction to $12,000, but lowers the tax benefits of itemized deductions. Depending on how you plan on filing your taxes, this may have lowered or raised your taxes.

LIST OF TAX CREDITS, CODES, BENEFITS, AND LAWS TO REDUCE YOUR TAX BURDEN

Standard deduction: This is a deduction the government gives you for just being you. The amount depends on your income, but it's in the thousands. If you're at least 65 by year's end, and your income is under $20,000 or so, the deduction is even higher.

Dependents: Each child you have is worth a deduction of about 4000. Nice going, kids!

State, local, and foreign taxes: It wouldn't make sense for the government to tax you twice on the same income, would it? Nope. So, you can deduct sales tax, property tax, and income taxes you've paid to your state city, or another country.

Donations to charity: You need a receipt or letter as proof. Your donation can be cash, physical things (like clothes or household stuff), expenses for volunteer work (like the gas to drive yourself there), or property (appraisal fees).

Profit from selling your house: Here's one of the last big tax shelters. If you made a profit from selling your home after living there at least two years, the first $250,000 of profit is yours, tax-free. (If you're married and filing jointly, make that $500,000.)

Hobby expenses: If you made money from a hobby (stamp collecting, antiquing, etc.), you can deduct what you spend on it.

Mortgage insurance premiums: Yep, if you pay mortgage insurance, you can deduct it.

Tax preparation: You can deduct what you pay someone to do your taxes, and the cost to file them electronically.

Social security taxes: If you're self-employed, and you've had to pay the 15.3 percent Social Security tax on your earnings, here's a little blessing: you can deduct half of it.

Tuition: Deduct up to 4000 you've paid for school (yours or your kid's).

The interest you've paid on mortgages and student loans: This one varies based on conditions we stated before.

Mortgage points: If you paid "points" to get your mortgage or building loan, you can deduct them.

Medical, dental, and nursing-home costs: If they're very high (over 10 percent of your income), you can even deduct the cost of renovations to your home if it was for medical reasons.

Expenses finding a job: Ads, agency fees, resume prep and printing, transportation to interviews, that kind of thing.

Moving expenses for a new job: Both moving companies and your own travel.

Travel expenses for military reservists: If you had to travel more than 100 miles for your service, you can deduct the travel, meals, and hotel.

Business use of your home: Home office? Inventory storage for your shop? Day care? Great! Deduct all these expenses you pay for the piece of your home. If the office is 15 percent of your home's square footage, then deduct 15 percent of the taxes, insurance, heating, cooling, electricity, maintenance, phone bills, depreciation, and so on.

Business use of your car: If driving is part of your job, great! Deduct your gas, parking, and insurance costs. If you don't feel like calculating all that, use 54 cents a mile (or whatever the 1 IRS current cents-per-mile allowance is).

Business travel expenses that your job doesn't reimburse you for. Planes, meals, hotels, laundry, the whole thing.

Employee expenses: If wining and dining clients is part of your job (entertainment, gifts, meals, driving), you can deduct some of it.

Education expenses: Yes, you can deduct up to $2500 per higher education student to pay for expenses like school supplies. Even if the student or a relative is paying those expenses in the first place!

Investment fees: If you pay an adviser, or you've paid a bank or broker to collect interest and dividends, you can deduct those payments.

Losses in your IRA: In the unlikely and terrible event that you cashed out your IRA or Roth IRA and got less than you put in, which you won't if you follow my guide, you can deduct the difference.

Income you gave back: If you were overpaid in a previous year and had to return some of the money, you can deduct what you gave back. Otherwise, it just wouldn't be fair

Certain legal fees: You can deduct lawyers' fees that involve either taxes or collecting money that you'll pay taxes on like what you paid a lawyer to get the alimony you're owed or attorney fees related to doing or keeping your job.

Safety-deposit box rentals: If you rented one of these boxes to store investments documents, you can deduct the rental fee.

Gambling losses: If you won some and lost some, you can deduct what you lost up to the amount you reported having won.

Disaster losses: If something bad happened to your house or car, you can deduct the losses that weren't covered by insurance.

Estate tax on an IRA: Someone rich who loves you passed away, which is very sad, but in his will, he left you his IRA, which is less sad. The estate was so big, the government charged estate tax, which is sad. But if you paid the estate tax on that IRA, you can deduct it, which is less sad.

Teacher's expenses: You, dear teacher, can deduct up to $250 for books, computers, and other teaching supplies that you weren't reimbursed for.

Health saving accounts (HSA): It is a special, tax exempt savings account that you can use to pay for medical expenses. And you can deduct what you pay into it.

Dependent care flexible spending account (FSA): Here's another special kind of savings account, this one containing fund you spend to take care of a child or a disabled spouse or parent. The first 5000 you put into this account is deductible.

Union dues including initiation fees

Uniforms for your job: You can deduct the cost of your uniforms (nurse, usher, surgeon, police officer) and even safety gear. Sorry, suits and dresses don't count as uniforms.

Alimony: If you must pay alimony to your ex, at least you don't have the pain of being taxed on that amount. Your ex gets to pay the taxes.

Health Insurance (if you're self-employed): Medical and dental, baby. Off the top, no limits.

Early-withdrawal penalties: If you withdrew money from a CD or some other time-fixed account and had to pay a penalty, you can deduct it.

Contributions to your IRA: Pay into that retirement account, dear reader. That's 5000 to 6500 you can deduct right off the top. (Roth IRA not included).

401k or SEP contributions: Anything you pay into this retirement account is deductible, too. SEP means a simplified employee pension - it is the retirement account of choice if you're self-employed.

Car registration: Yep, in some situation, you can deduct what you paid for your car's license.

Jury-duty pay: Ok, so you served on a jury. After the first few days, the court paid you the tiny amount that they pay jurors. But your boss is enlightened and cool (or lives in a state with laws about this sort of thing) and paid your salary anyway. In that case, you don't get to keep both your salary and what the court paid you; you must give your boss the jury-duty pay. You can deduct that money from your income

Bad debts: If you lent out money and there's no chance of getting it back, then you can deduct it – and you can learn a lesson.

The magic of the tax credit is, "Are you getting 'em all?" There's a big difference between a tax deduction and a tax credit. A deduction lowers the amount of income you use to calculate your taxes. Suppose, for example, that you pay 30 percent of your income in taxes. If you made $1000 this year (well done!) and you get a $100 deduction, then you'll be taxed as if you earned only $9000. You'll pay $270 instead of $300. The tax deductions saved you $30. A tax credit subtracts money from your taxes, not your income. If you made $1,000 this year, and you get a 100-dollar tax credit, then your taxes will be 200 instead of 300. The tax credit saved you 100. Therefore, missing out on a tax credit is a big boo-boo. Make sure you know them all! As usual, these are only pointers; there are footnotes and limits on most of them.

Earned income tax credit: The EITC is meant to help people earning less than $50,000 or so, especially working parents with children. The amount you get varies according to your income and number of kids, but it's worth between 500 and 6200 dollars

Child-care credit: If you pay someone to take care of your kid while you're at work - like a nanny, preschool, daycare, before- or after-school care, or event summer day camp, you can get 20 to 35 percent of that money as a tax credit. Maximum credit is 1050 for one kid, or 2100 for two or more. It's for kids under 13, but it's also available if you paid someone to care for an adult who is incapable of self-care.

Child credit Kids: They're the gifts that keep on giving. If you earn less than 75 or 110k if you're married and filing jointly, you can subtract 1000 per kid from your taxes. You can still get this credit if you earn more than that, but the credit drops by 50 for every 1000 you make over the 75k threshold.

Saver's tax credit: Your government really, really wants you to save for retirement. The savers tax credit is intended for low to middle income workers - those earning less than 60k (married couple filing jointly), 45000 (head of household) or 30k for everyone else.

Retirement Savings tax credit: If you manage to sock away some money for retirement, you can subtract the amount from what you own in taxes. If all goes well, in fact, this credit can reduce your tax all the way down to zero. You can deduct either 50 percent, 20 percent, or 10 percent of your retirement account contribution, depending on your income. For example, suppose you're married (it could happen) and together you and your spouse make 35k a year. Each of you then socks away 1000 into a retire account. Just like a 401 or IRA, you can subtract 50 percent of what you owe in taxes for this. A handy 1000 IRS discount.

American Opportunity Credit: If you earn less than 80k or 160k filing jointly, then you can get up to 2.5k in tax credits for money you're paying for someone's college bills every year. If your income is higher, you get a smaller amount back. If you like, you may prefer the Lifetime Learning Credit, which is similar, it gives you back 20 percent of what you spend to go back to school yourself, for any reason, at any school. The credit is 2000 tops. (You can't claim both of these credits in the same year.) This one is available if you earn less than 6k a year (a 130k married).

Alternative energy credit: Have you blessed your home with the installation of clean-energy system like solar water heaters, geothermal heat pumps, or wind turbines? The IRS thanks you- by kicking back 30 percent of the total cost, including labor. That is one huge warm credit. And that's why I believe getting solar panels makes sense from an investment stand point. It also reduces another bill which lowers our monthly expenses. This, in turn, brings us closer and quicker towards financially freedom and independence.

Traditional energy upgrades: Even if you upgrade your home's non-effective energy systems, the government will refund 10 percent of the cost up to 500 in credit. That covers heat pumps, central air conditioning, water heaters, furnaces, insulation, roofs, windows, doors, and skylights.

You may or may not notice, but I have not once mentioned the words "tax refund." The reason why I never accounted for the tax refund in any section is because someone reading this book may currently have tax issues or an extremely low tax refund, and it wouldn't be fair to budget a tax return into any budget or allocation. It does go without saying that any money that you receive from a tax refund will and should go to paying off debt, building up your emergency fund or rainy-day fund, investing, or used to further or start your business.

I also want to quickly state that it is almost always beneficial to file your taxes jointly if you're married compared to filing separately. If you're wondering the fringe scenarios when it isn't better, please check out this guide: https://turbotax.intuit.com/tax-tips/marriage/should-you-and-your-spouse-file-taxes-jointly-or-separately/L7gyjnqyM.

I just want to state that if you have tax issues or any questions regarding taxes, please seek a tax expert.

CHAPTER 7
LIFE TIPS

BUY EXPERIENCES, NOT THINGS

If you are following this guide religiously, you will become financially free and independent and find yourself loaded with plenty of money. You've been saving this whole time and you want to spend some of it, and to be frank, you deserve it! What I recommend that you spend your money on is experiences and not things. Let's take for example that you always wanted a Tesla car, so you decide to get one. The Tesla car will bring you some type of happiness for a couple of weeks, but eventually it will get old and cease to bring you happiness like it once did.

Personally, instead of spending 25-50k on a new car, I would rather spend 25-50k on a lavish vacation for a week, once a month, over the course of a year. Think about how many long-lasting memories this could potentially generate! I would suggest taking this money and spending on a skill or something that you've always wanted to do. Which one do you think will make you happier: the car or literally traveling the world and seeing the different cultures of this world? I'm not just talking out my ass about this, there is literal research to back up the claim that experiences, not things, make you happy. A link to that study is below:

Link to guide: https://www.lifehack.org/294156/studies-show-that-people-who-buy-experiences-not-things-are-happier

CONSIDER BEING HEALTHIER

I highly recommend that you consider one of these dietary choices: vegan, vegetarian, or pescatarian. What I am about to say is a fact and not opinion, People who live the longest are pescatarians, vegans, and vegetarians in that order. If you don't want to go vegan, vegetarian, or pescatarian, I understand, but I still recommend cutting out almost all red meat from your diet and replacing it with fruits and vegetables. You will need to be around for a while to spend all that money that you have saved up! I am not your dietarian, please seek a dietarian if you want to make serious changes to your diet. I am merely giving my opinion on what a healthy diet consists of.

WAIT TO HAVE KIDS

I highly suggest waiting to have kids. Every year you put off having kids, easily puts an extra 15k in your bank account that you can use to become financially free and independent at a quicker rate. I didn't just make that number up either; that is a direct quote from the Department of Agriculture: "The estimated cost of raising a child from birth through age 17 is $233,610 -- or as much as almost $14,000 annually". This statistic is the average for a middle-income couple. It's a bit more expensive in urban parts of the country, and less so in rural areas.

Let's face it, kids are expensive because there are so many hidden costs people don't even think about before having them. Now, I'm not telling you not to have kids at all because kids are true blessings and give people purpose in life. All I am saying is, if possible, push back having kids before the pressures of starting a family kick in.

GET A SPOUSE THAT IS WITH YOUR PLAN TO REACH FINANCIAL FREEDOM AND INDEPENDENCE

If you're not married and currently dating someone, please consider what type of person that you would want in a life partner. For example, if your girlfriend or boyfriend is terrible with money and figuratively sets his paycheck on fire every month, do you think that this person would realistically be okay with following this guide or following a budget detailed in this book? Nothing is harder than living with someone who undermines your goals. It will be borderline impossible to accomplish your financial goals if your spouse spends all your money or all their money and comes to you for more. I'm not saying these types of people don't deserve to be married; they just may not be the right type of person for you if you intend to take the principles of this book seriously.

If you are already married, I would ask your partner to read this book or at least the section talking about investments to get them interested or excited about saving and reaching financial freedom and independence. Get a spouse that is supportive of all your dreams, especially your financial dreams and in return be supportive of all their dreams as well.

WORK OUT

I'll be frank with you, I hate working out and exercising. You know why I force myself to work out anyway? Working out teaches the body how to push through adversary and, believe it or not, it will make it easier to follow the principles of this book. I know it sounds crazy, but I shit you not. Start working out regularly and tell me if you don't seem like you have more self-control with just about every aspect of your life. The additional benefits of working out are that it keeps you healthier, happier, and feeling more satisfied with life. It'll also keep your spouse happier to know that their significant other is in great shape. I understand love isn't about physicality, but who doesn't want their significant other to have a smoking hot body? I'll leave a link for beginners who want to start working out, but just don't know where to start.

Beginners Guide to working out: https://www.theo.fit/blog/beginnerlift

MEDITATE

The way I look at meditating, it's like exercising for the brain. Meditating teaches you to be more present in everyday life so that you're not worried about things in the past or the future. What I do is wake up 15 minutes early before I would typically start my day and go outside to meditate and clear my mind. Not only does it allow me to get some vitamin D by bathing in the sunlight, but also it allows me to make more rational calm decisions during the day. If you're iffy on if you want to meditate, I say try meditating for 30 days straight and if you don't feel better, stop. You want to keep your mind, soul, and body in the best shape possible so that you can reap the hard work that you have put in to become financially free by living a quality life as long as possible

TRAVEL

This is one of the only things I recommend spending your money on. There is a huge world out there that has so many awesome people, places, wonders, and food just waiting for you to go and try them. Traveling the world will give you a whole different perspective of the world and the people in it. Every culture and people have amazing qualities and ways of living that you have never considered before. I recommend putting money in your budget every month to take a vacation to a new location every year. It will change your outlook on life. Nobody ever died and said "damn, I wish I wouldn't have traveled around the world." The amazing experiences and memories you will make traveling will literally stick with you for the rest of your life. There's a whole world out there waiting for you to explore it.

DON'T BE AFRAID TO TRY

Please don't be afraid of trying. If you are scared to do something and you are feeling overwhelmed about anything in life, just take the first step. I guarantee that once you do this, you will realize that it's not half as bad as you thought. No man can be blamed for trying and failing, but a man can be blamed for not trying at all. As long as you live your life trying to accomplish your goals and your dreams, you can live your life knowing that you gave it your all. Remember the secret to being rich, wealthy, owning your own business, and accomplishing your dreams and your goals is taking the first step towards it. If you take the first step and you remain consistent you will eventually accomplish the task or goals that you have for yourself. If you have enough dedication, drive, and consistency there's literally nothing stopping you from doing anything that you want to do.

CHAPTER 8
LEGACY PROTECTION

OPENING A TRUST

A trust is a tool for dividing ownership of property between legal title and beneficial enjoyment. The holder of legal title is called the trustee and is responsible for managing the property, based on the terms of the trust, for the benefit of the named beneficiary of the trust. Some trusts are revocable because you can change your mind at any time about who the beneficiaries are, or you can take the property out of the trust entirely. Trusts that don't allow you to change the terms once the trust has been established are irrevocable trusts. The distinction between revocable versus irrevocable trusts is very important, since some types of trusts won't work if you set them up with the wrong kind of revocability.

The moment you turn the assets over to the trustee, you are no longer the legal owner of those assets. Therefore, it is a way to keep assets away from those who sue you. Keep in mind, however, that for this potent asset protection feature to kick in, you must create an irrevocable trust. This means, you cannot directly change the terms of the trust deed once the trust has been set up. If a court determines that you still exercise considerable control over the trust assets, it can order you to turn those assets over to a creditor or a plaintiff.

A bypass trust is designed to help married couples avoid unnecessary estate tax liability. Each spouse sets up their estate planning documents to leave property up to the maximum allowed under the estate tax exclusion to the bypass trust, then bequeaths the rest of what they own to the other spouse. Property left to one's spouse qualifies for a marital deduction to the estate tax, so when one spouse dies, the other can get the bequeathed property tax-free.

Meanwhile, the property left to the trust is covered by the estate tax exclusion, but it's also not subject to estate tax in the surviving spouse's estate. So as the property increases in value, it can safely grow above the exclusion amount without incurring potential estate tax at the death of the surviving spouse.

The terms of the bypass trust generally allow the surviving spouse to get support from the trust, although it's typically better to spend down other assets that will be included in the surviving spouse's estate. When the surviving spouse dies, the contents of the trust go to the named beneficiaries, who can then get it without facing an additional round of estate taxes. A link with more information about estates and trust is below:

https://www.investopedia.com/articles/pf/12/set-up-a-trust-fund.asp

TEACH YOUR KIDS ABOUT INVESTING AS EARLY AS POSSIBLE

Please teach your kids about investing from a young age. I understand young kids may not have the interest or the patience to get excited about a potential 8% a year, because when you're a kid you can't even wait till the end of dinner for a cookie. One skill from the book below is on how to get your kid excited about investing: The method is to simulate an accelerated interest rate to keep them interested. So, for example we are going to open the Bank of Dad where if your kids put money with you, they can get 10% a month or 10% a week. This will teach them the power of using money to make money.

Take them to your rental properties from a young age and give them a piece of the rental property money for helping you "manage" the property with them. If you own a business, have them work the business for a time even if that job is "management." I also recommend at the age of thirteen put your kids as a user on your credit cards to start building their credit and start teaching them some of the key components of credit such as, how to properly manage credit cards, the importance of paying attention to your credit score. If there's something your kid is super passionate about like a clothing brand, game company, etc., buy them some stock in that company and tell them that all the gains it makes is theirs. I really recommend reading the book *A Complete Investing Guide for Kids* for so more tips like this. I guarantee you that it's a great read. If you can't find it at the library or "online," it's well worth the 10-20 dollars it will take the buy it. A link to buy the book is below:

https://www.amazon.com/Growing-Money-Complete-Investing-Guide/dp/0843199059/ref=sr_1_1?keywords=A+Complete+Investing+Guide+for+Kids&qid=1563515594&s=gateway&sr=8-1

MAKE SURE TO HELP OTHER FAMILY MEMBERS

If you follow and implemented the principles of this book, you have the secret on how to be out of debt and become financially free and independent. Teach as many people as possible that will listen about the principles of this book. Help them make budgets, teach them how to create a smart investment portfolio, and teach them the power of getting out of debt and why they should strive to reach financial freedom and independence. You should want your family members to be as financially successfully as you. Passing on your knowledge of finances and investing will help your family create generational wealth.

CONCLUSION

Over the course of this book, you have challenged the status quo of American consumerism, the concept of living a life you can't afford, and learned that the Joneses are truly broke. You also learned and mastered the 16 steps to financial freedom, which include getting a job that makes sense, saving for a rainy-day fund, keeping some emergency money, creating a life-changing budget, paying off debt, buying a starter home, and investing a total of at least 15% pretax of your income.

Further, you learned about buying and renting out multiple starter homes, creating and owning a business that you truly are passionate about, achieving and maintaining excellent credit, and gaining financial independence and freedom to where you have more passive income than expenses. You are now continuing to invest and acquire more and more rental properties until you have enough passive income to replace your salary. You have learned how to master money and make it work for you instead of you working for your money. You now have a responsibility to spread the concepts of this book to as many people as possible.

Think about how many lives you can change with the knowledge that you now know about money and finances. If you have been following this book religiously, you have at a minimum excellent credit, three paid off houses, you are worth at least a million dollars, making close to if not 100,000 dollars, you have 10-20k in a money market account or savings account, and have absolutely no debt. If you're in a similar situation to me, you would have 8 million dollars in investments, at least 5 million dollars in real estate, and at least $300,000 in passive income annually.

You have created an amazing investment portfolio that accounts for nearly everything: traditional markets, nontraditional markets, commodities, yourself, cash, and real estate. Your investment portfolio has a good mix of low, medium, and high-risk reward relationships. Our investment strategy is set up so that the lower the risk, the higher the allocation is in our portfolio. You no longer are thinking about the American dream; you have become the American dream. You are part of the 3% of people in America that don't have to work a job anymore, because you have more passive income than expenses.

You now have the skills to not only master money, but to master your life as well. Not only are you financially free, but also you are now doing what you love to do, when you want to do it, and you can choose how much you want to do it, because you have the luxury of being financially free. Go forward and live your life that is now full of abundance of everything that you have ever wanted such as money, happiness, and experiences. The world is your oyster and now you have the techniques and skills to do anything you want.

I just want to state that I am so proud of you for deciding to take your life and your finances into your own hands. You have followed this guide and become financially free and broken the generational curse placed on your lineage of being financially illiterate. You are now armed with all the information needed to teach a proven strategy to change people's lives. You have the knowledge to transform a person that literally has nothing and teach them the steps to reach financial freedom. I am passing the torch of learning onto you, to go out and teach as many people as humanly possible the right way to manage, handle, and invest money. This guide was created to be a fool-proof plan for the common man to reach financial independence and financial freedom. Please go out of your way to teach as many people the financial principles of this book, because you could change someone's financial future for the better.

The knowledge of this book should be taught by schools and governments, but unfortunately being financially literate is not seen as important. You've heard the millennium old saying that "give a man a fish and he eats for a day, but teach a man to fish and he eats for a lifetime."

This saying is extremely applicable to finance; you can't really blame a person or a family that hasn't been taught how to be financially literate for making bad financial decisions. The point of this book is to give everybody the knowledge necessary to become financially free and independent. You should give back by giving your knowledge, time, energy, and/or resources. Nothing makes the human soul happier than giving back. You now have the knowledge, time, energy, and resources to make a difference in someone's life.

ACKNOWLEDGEMENTS

I want to thank my dad, Kevin Coleman, for giving me the basis of my investing knowledge and allowing me to have open discussions about finances in their home. Instead of snuffing out my ideas of writing a book about becoming financially free and independent, He was instead supporting and encouraging me to get my ideas about the subject out into the world. This book wouldn't have been created without his constant support and advice.

My mom also supported my dream of becoming financially free and independent from an early age. She was the one who showed me how to be financially frugal and how to stick to a budget.

I also want to acknowledge Dave Ramsey for helping me understand the basics when it comes to money management and finances through his books and his seminars. I honestly believe he is one of the best financial advisors out there, because his message is constantly clear and concise.

I want to give a special shout-out to my sister and my brother for supporting me in my journey of writing this book, and giving constant support, criticism, and advice when it comes to writing this book.

Lastly, I truly appreciate all the business owners that allowed me to interview them about their struggles with owning a business and tips for owning one. Your stories and advice have inspired me and convinced me that I am going about the right path towards being financially free and independent.

INDEX AND LIST OF RECOMMENDED FINANCIAL TOOLS/ACCOUNTS/WEBSITES THROUGHOUT THE GUIDE:

Link to Cheap and Free Text Books: https://campustechnology.com/articles/2013/08/14/the-price-is-right-11-excellent-sites-for-free-digital-textbooks.aspx

Link to more well-paying trade jobs and jobs you can get out college: https://www.onlinecollegeplan.com/vocational-school-highest-paying-careers/

Link to how to easily get your GED:

https://bestgedclasses.org/how-to-get-ged/

Link to Dave Ramsey's Approach to Money:

https://www.daveramsey.com/blog/the-number-one-way-credit-score

Link to Mint Budgeting App Guide:

https://www.mint.com/budgeting-3/how-to-create-a-budget-using-mint

Link to 529 College Plan for more education:

https://www.savingforcollege.com/intro-to-529s/what-is-a-529-plan

Link to Car Buying Guide:

https://www.consumerreports.org/buying-a-car/used-car-buying-guide/

Link to CarFax:

https://www.carfax.com/

Link to Best Checking Accounts: https://www.nerdwallet.com/blog/banking/nerdwallets-top-online-checking-accounts/

Link to Best Money Market Accounts: https://www.nerdwallet.com/blog/banking/best-money-market-accounts/?trk=nw_gn2_4.0

Link to Debt Repayment Calculator:

http://www.finaid.org/calculators/prepayment.phtml.

A guide to using personal capital for portfolio allocation tracking:

https://investorjunkie.com/43696/started-personal-capital/

Link to 401k valuation over a period of time:

https://www.bankrate.com/calculators/retirement/401-k-retirement-calculator.aspx

Link to betterment: https://www.betterment.com/start-investing/?dd_pm=none&dd_pm_cat=brokerage&dd_pm_company=betterment

Link to estimate how much you will have at retirement for a non-401k retirement account: https://www.nerdwallet.com/investing/roth-ira-calculator

Straight comparison of a traditional 401k and a Roth IRA: https://www.calcxml.com/calculators/ret10?skn=#results

How to protect your precious metals and silver from theft: https://www.youtube.com/watch?v=SXFLZub7DaU

Link to M1 finance website: https://www.m1finance.com/ Link to

Joseph Carlson's high yield dividend investing portfolio

https://urlzs.com/U45YH

Link with examples or data that shows how dividend stocks outperform index funds: https://www.thebalance.com/why-dividend-stocks-outperform-non-dividend-stocks-357353

Link that provides you a calculator to see how much passive

income you can generate from initial investment of 25,000 dollars: https://www.investopedia.com/calculator/dvcal.aspx

Link to coinbase: www.coinbase.com

Ledger from amazon with the below link: https://www.amazon.com/s?k=ledger+nano+s&crid=1WUH7CVED39OR&sprefix=ledger+%2Caps%2C196&ref=nb_sb_ss_i_2_7

Follow the below guide to learn how to put cryptocurrency from coinbase to your ledger:

Link: https://www.chainbits.com/cryptocurrencies/how-to-transfer-cryptocurrency/

Link to 4 year hold strategies YouTube channel: https://www.youtube.com/channel/UC0zGwzu0zzCImC1BwPuWyXQ

Links to both AngeList and SeedInvest: https://angel.co/ and https://www.seedinvest.com/.

Link to buying homes: https://lifehacker.com/the-start-to-finish-guide-to-buying-a-home-1663317601

Zillow, Truila, and home finder. Here are the links to these websites: https://www.zillow.com/ and https://www.trulia.com/ and https://homefinder.com/

Links for tips and things to ask for while negotiating during mortgage talks: https://www.theglobeandmail.com/real-estate/mortgages-and-rates/the-ultimate-mortgage-checklist-63-steps-to-navigating-the-best-deal/article14868520/

Link to how to structure and manage a month-to-month lease: https://www.rocketlawyer.com/article/how-a-month-to-month-rental-agreement-works-cb.rl

Link to early loan payment calculator: https://www.bankrate.com/calculators/mortgages/mortgage-loan-payoff-calculator.aspx

Link to buying your first rental property: https://fitsmallbusiness.com/buying-your-first-rental-property-tips/

A link to check what interest rates you can expect in your country is below. It has monthly updates to help the below information stay relevant: https://www.bankrate.com/mortgage.aspx.

Link to being a good landlord: https://www.landlordology.com/first-time-landlord-tips/ and Guide to getting good tenants:https://www.thebalancesmb.com/the-right-tenant-for-your-rental-2124984

Link to rental property management: https://learn.roofstock.com/blog/how-much-do-property-managers-charge

Link to negotiating a raise is below: http://techgenix.com/negotiating-a-raise/

Link to net worth calculator: https://www.nerdwallet.com/blog/finance/net-worth-calculator/

Links to some good Freelancing Sites: Fiverr: https://www.fiverr.com/ and Upwork: https://www.upwork.com/ and Cloud peeps: https://www.cloudpeeps.com/

Link to the right way to be an uber or lyft driver: https://www.ridester.com/maximize-uber-earnings/

Link to RockStarflippersyoutube guide is below: https://www.youtube.com/watch?v=Xc4OjVDFmyA&list=PLofXh8bXBtpWYTGHSP0iAxVQD9icXD7v6

Link to RockStarflippersyoutube guide is below: https://www.youtube.com/watch?v=Xc4OjVDFmyA&list=PLofXh8bXBtpWYTGHSP0iAxVQD9icXD7v6

Link to Vending Machine Guide: https://www.youtube.com/watch?v=Saqk1kfhJBE

Link to 99 potential side hustles: https://www.sidehustlenation.com/ideas/

A link on how to obtain a business license: https://www.wikihow.com/Obtain-a-Business-License

A link to find what permits you need for your business is below: https://www.sba.gov/business-guide/launch-your-business/apply-licenses-permits

Guide to health insurance: https://www.nerdwallet.com/blog/health/health-insurance-guide/

The below link finds the best possible prices for long-term care insurance in your area: https://www.reviews.com/life-insurance/long-term-care/. I

If you want more information about long-term care insurance, please check out this website: https://www.nerdwallet.com/blog/insurance/long-term-care-insurance/

Link to Qapital: https://www.qapital.com/

Link to Solar Panel Calculator:https://news.energysage.com/how-much-does-the-average-solar-panel-installation-cost-in-the-u-s/

Link to Solar City: https://www.tesla.com/solarpanels?energy_redirect=true

Link to guide on how to sell energy back to your electric company: https://solartechonline.com/blog/net-metering-how-to-sell-residential-solar-power-back-to-the-utility-company/

Link to his website: https://clark.com/ .

Link to *Pogue's Basics: Money* is below if you're interested in buying and reading the book: https://urlzs.com/ygdEy

If you're wondering about the fringe scenarios when it isn't better, please check out this guide: https://turbotax.intuit.com/tax-tips/marriage/should-you-and-your-spouse-file-taxes-jointly-or-separately/L7gyjnqyM.

Link to guide: https://www.lifehack.org/294156/studies-show-that-people-who-buy-experiences-not-things-are-happier

Beginners Guide to working out: https://www.theo.fit/blog/beginnerlift

A link with more information about estates and trust is below: https://www.investopedia.com/articles/pf/12/set-up-a-trust-fund.asp

Link to buy the book: https://www.amazon.com/Growing-Money-Complete-Investing-Guide/dp/0843199059/ref=sr_1_1?keywords=A+Complete+Investing+Guide+for+Kids&qid=1563515594&s=gateway&sr=8-1

If you want more information when it comes to turning your vacation house into a rental property, please use the guide below: https://www.washingtonian.com/2016/02/18/you-can-find-renters-to-pay-off-your-vacation-house-airbnb-vrbo-homeaway/

If you want more information when it comes to turning your rental properties into AirbNbs, please see this link: https://www.passiveairbnb.com/airbnb-hosting-guide/

If you're interested in rent-to-own and want more information, a link is below: https://www.trulia.com/guides/how-does-rent-to-own-work/

If you have more questions about social security, the link below contains more information: https://www.kiplinger.com/article/retirement/T051-C032-S014-5-steps-to-maximize-your-social-security-benefit.html

Link for SEP IRA: https://clark.com/personal-finance-credit/what-is-a-sep-ira/

If you're interested in more information about Medicare, please read this link for more information: https://www.kiplinger.com/slideshow/retirement/T039-S001-7-things-medicare-doesnt-cover/index.html)

BOOK REFERENCES

"*Intelligent Investor*" by Warren Buffet

The Founder's Dilemmas by Noam Wasserman

"*Millionare Dollar Mindset*" by Chris Hogan

"*Pogues Basics: Money*" by David Pogue

A Complete Investing Guide for Kids

www.ingramcontent.com/pod-product-compliance
Lightning Source LLC
Chambersburg PA
CBHW020903180526
45163CB00007B/2613